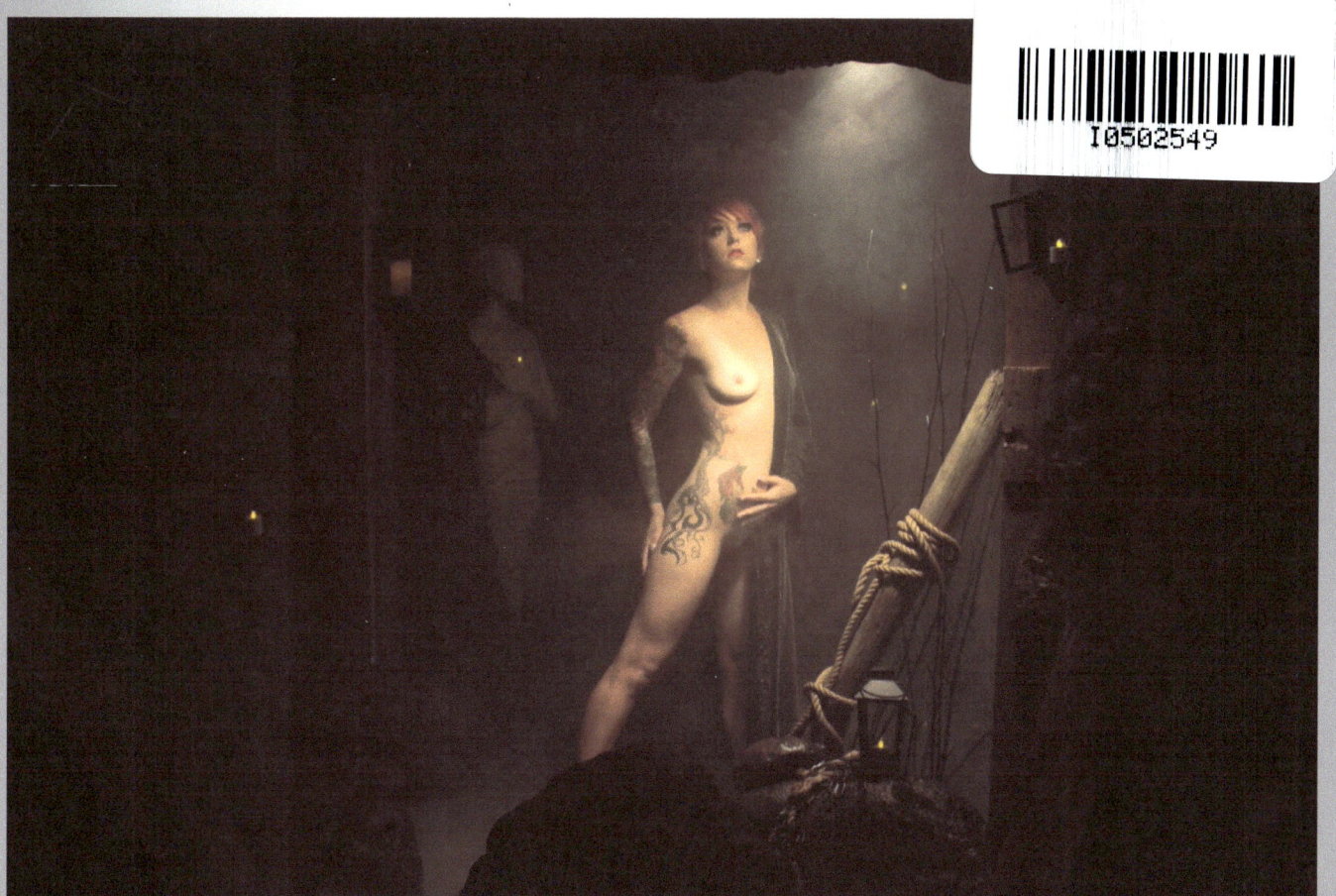

In this the third book of my art nude series we look upon images showing the tattoo art of the models

To be comfortable in one's skin is a rare commodity. Art nudes have been popular since painting was discovered and although art photography had to endure much more scrutiny, there is no denying the impact a nude picture can create. The intense sexuality and expression inside a frozen frame can ultimately leave any spectator speechless. Now add the tattoo's influence.

The human body in its natural form can be defined as one of the most beautiful objects in the world. Each one is unique yet similar. Tattoos allow this beautiful object to become a canvas for numerous ways of expression. These drawings, either colorful or plain, let the individual exhibit a piece of what they are thinking or feeling with stunning visual effects. In combination with nude photography the promise to capture and inspire is never left wanting.

The biggest connection between the two has to be freedom. The freedom to decorate and the freedom to express have created so much controversy around the world, thus reaching the goal it aims for. Endless discussions which are purely based on whether nudity and tattoo's represent mere physical arousal or something much deeper can be heard in almost every language.

Art nudes and ink have formed part of a movement that cannot be described with words or thoughts. The elements involved is too complex and do not conform to what can be said, but rather with what it inspires. Whether it renders the spectator uneasy or uncomfortable, the fact remains there is an effect.

For those who do enjoy this freedom, few things can compare. Skin holds much more beauty than clothes ever will. Utilizing the best canvas in the world with ink projections that is buried in the roots of so many cultures across the globe, can only end in what is known as art.

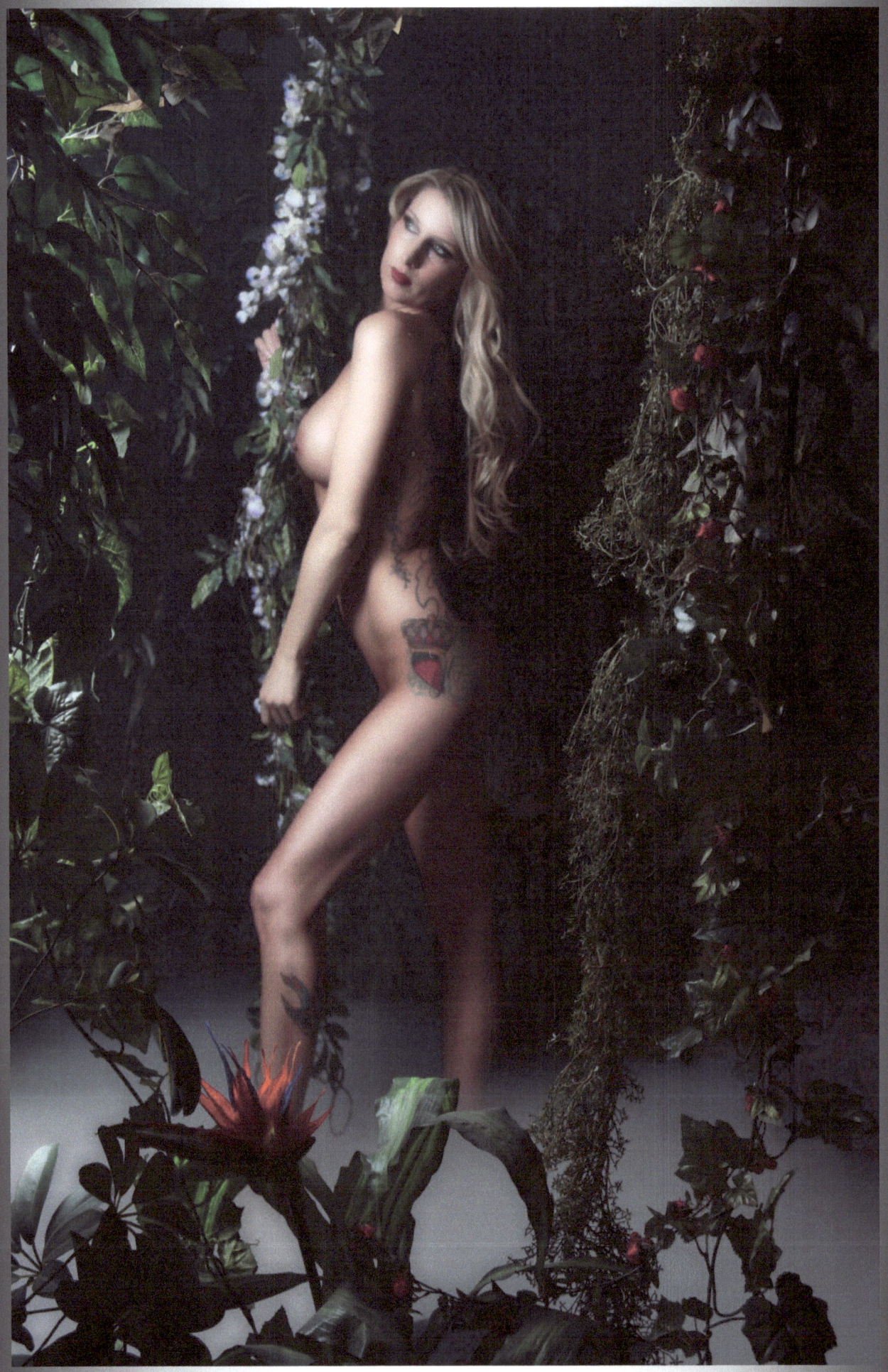

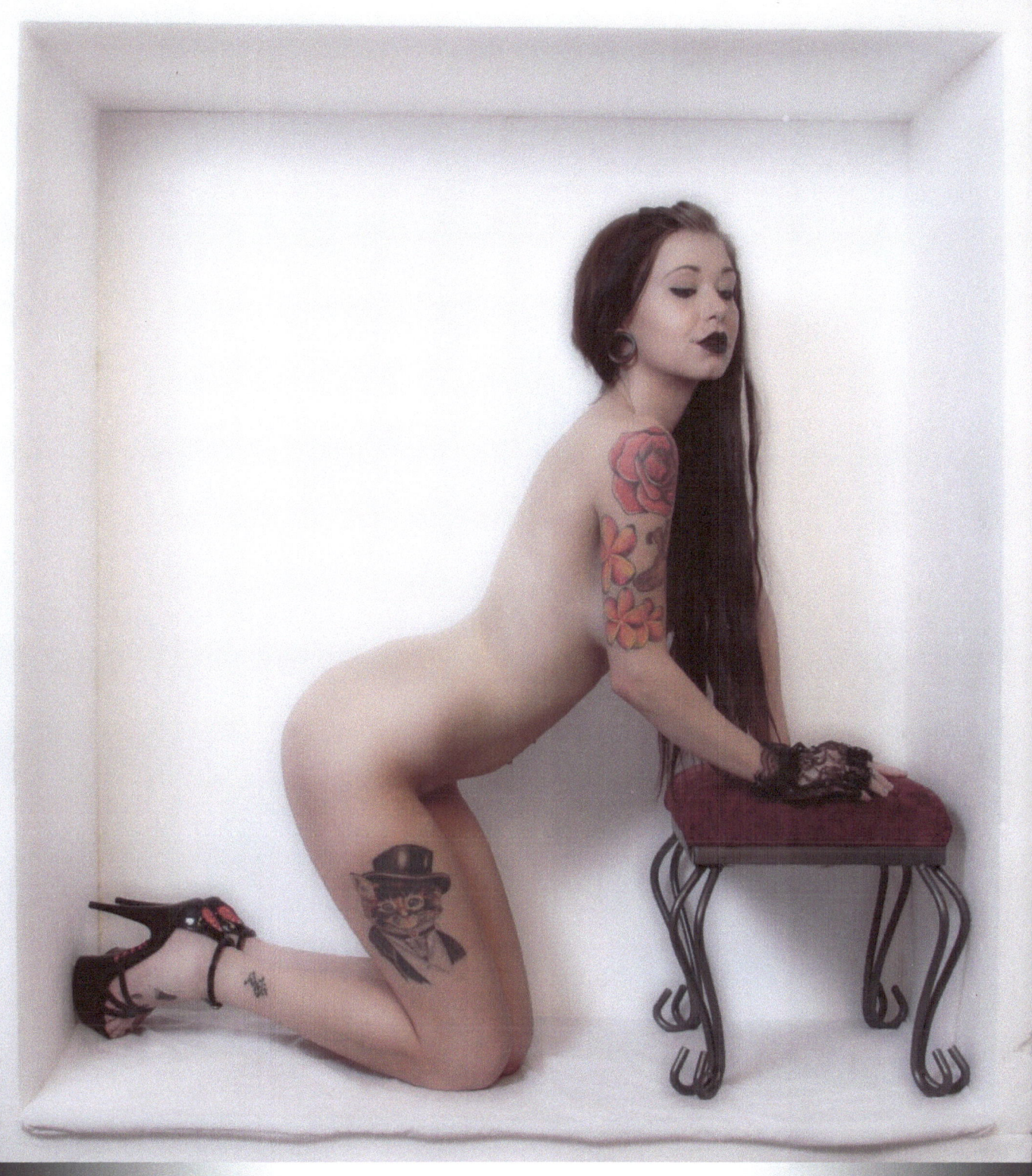

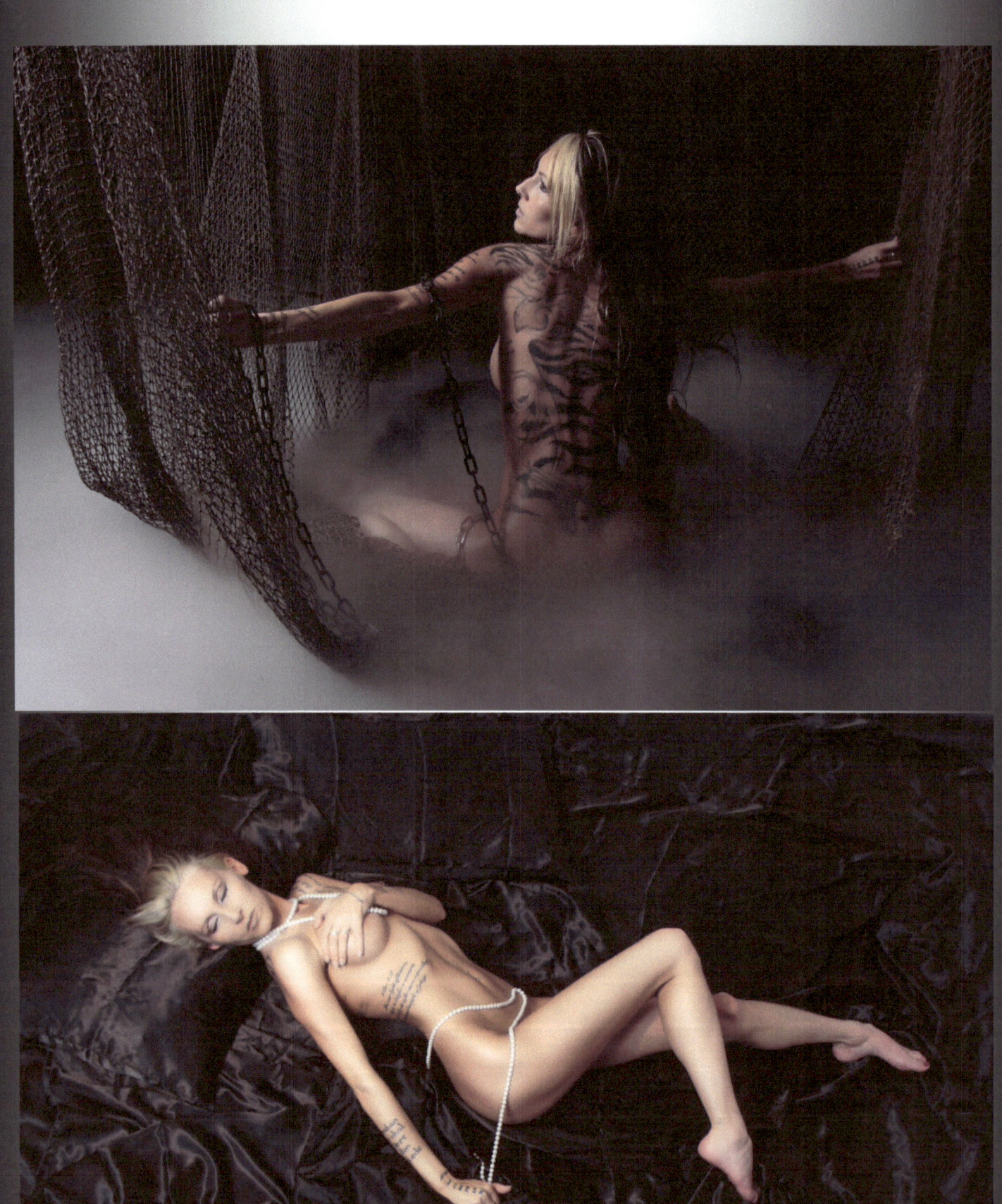

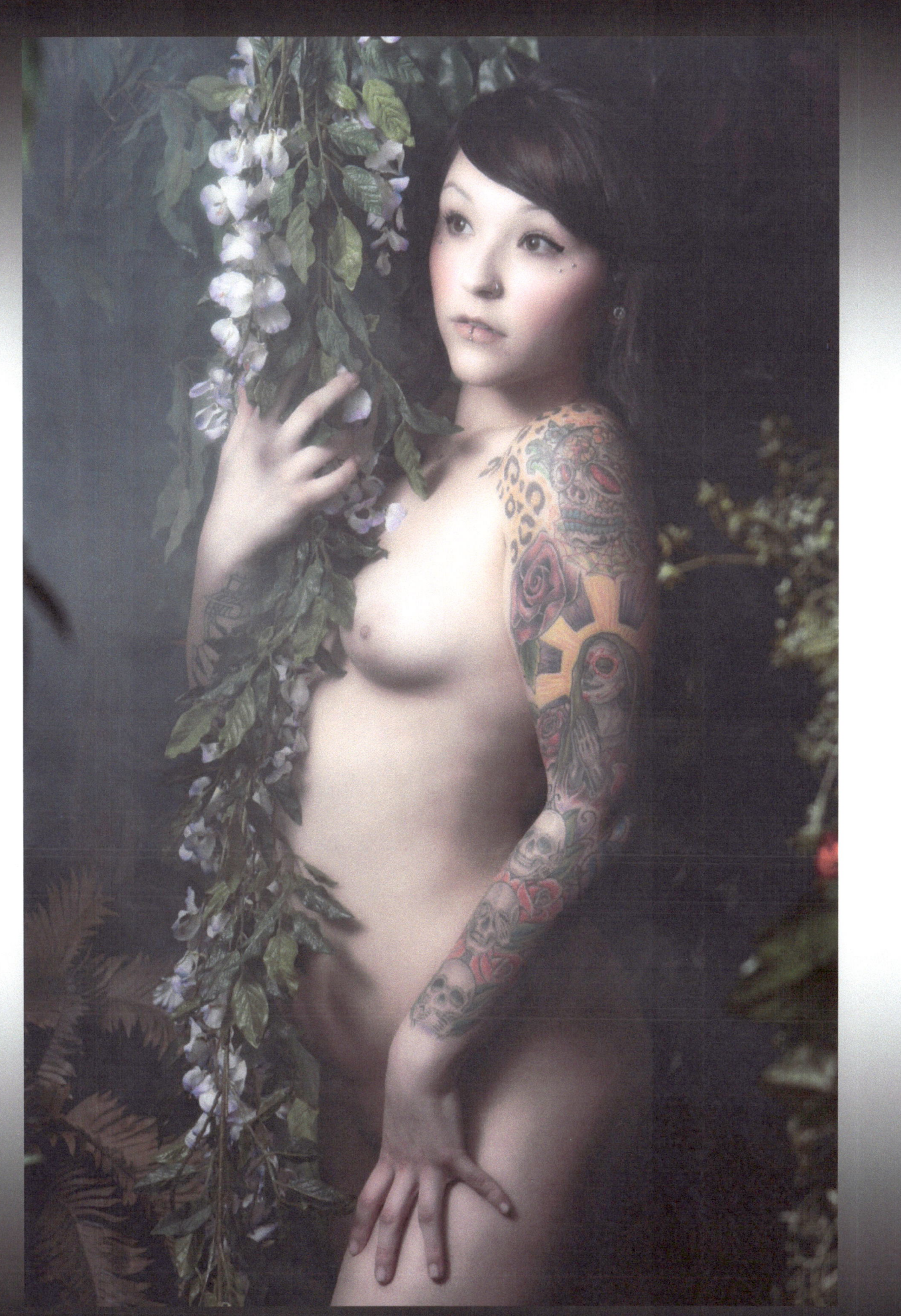

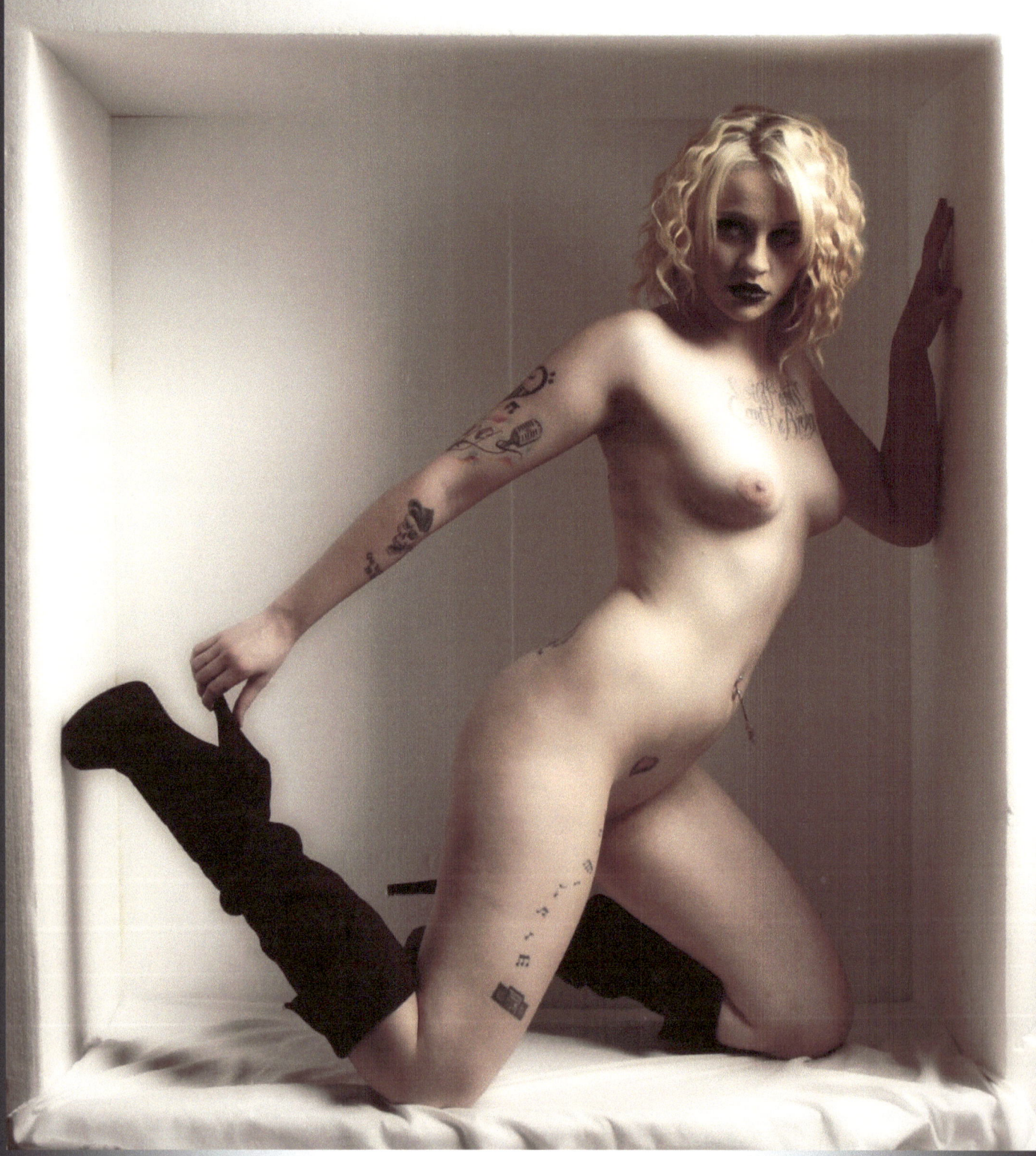

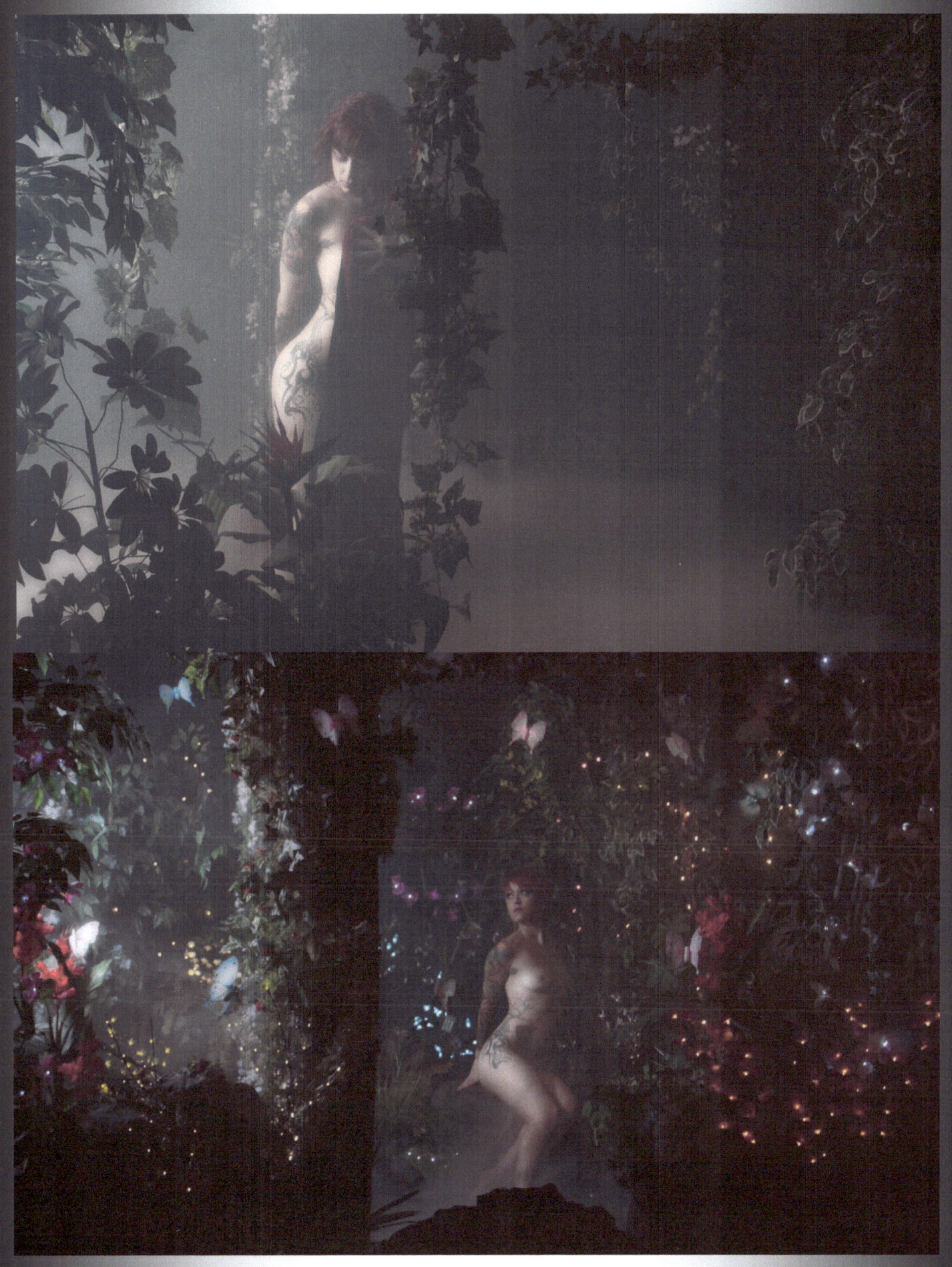

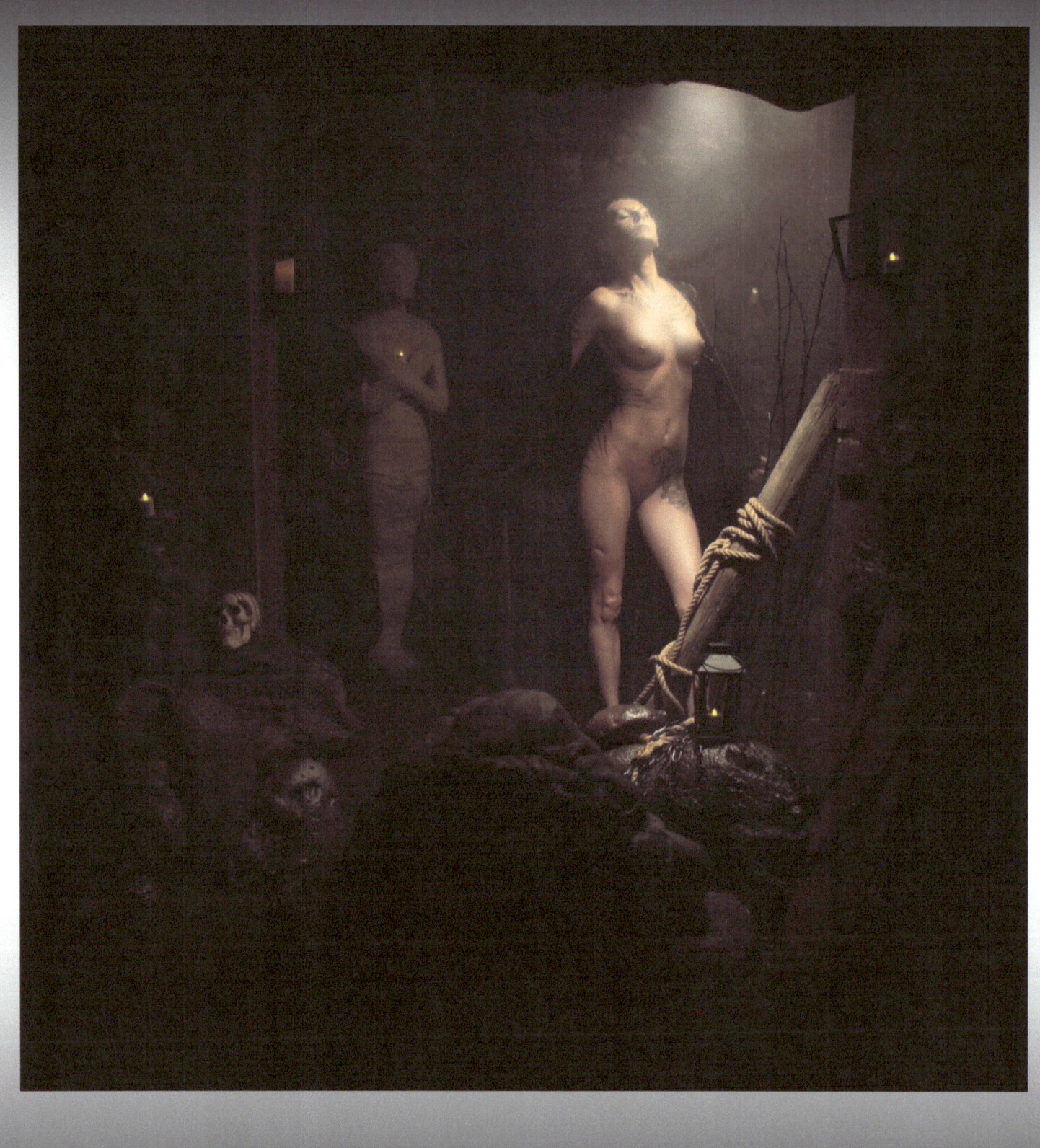

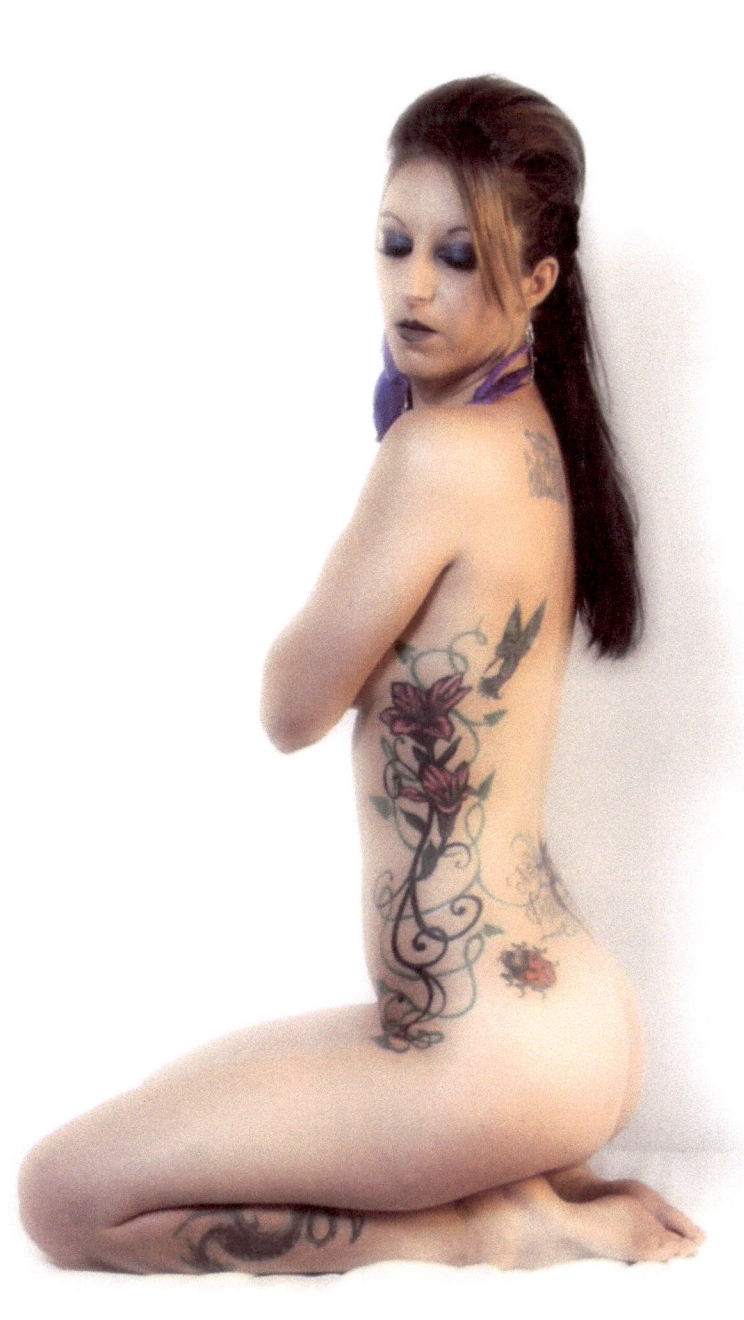

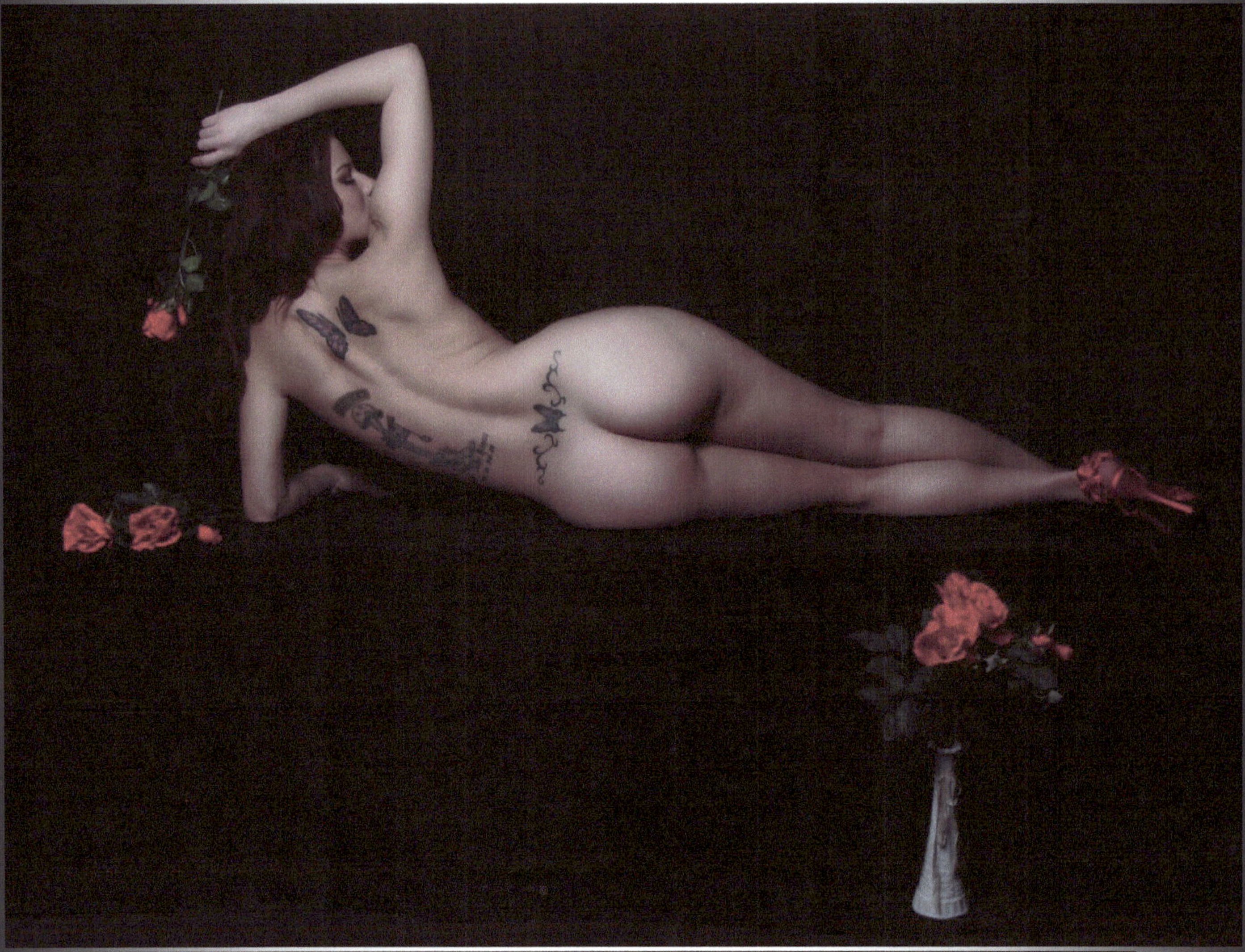

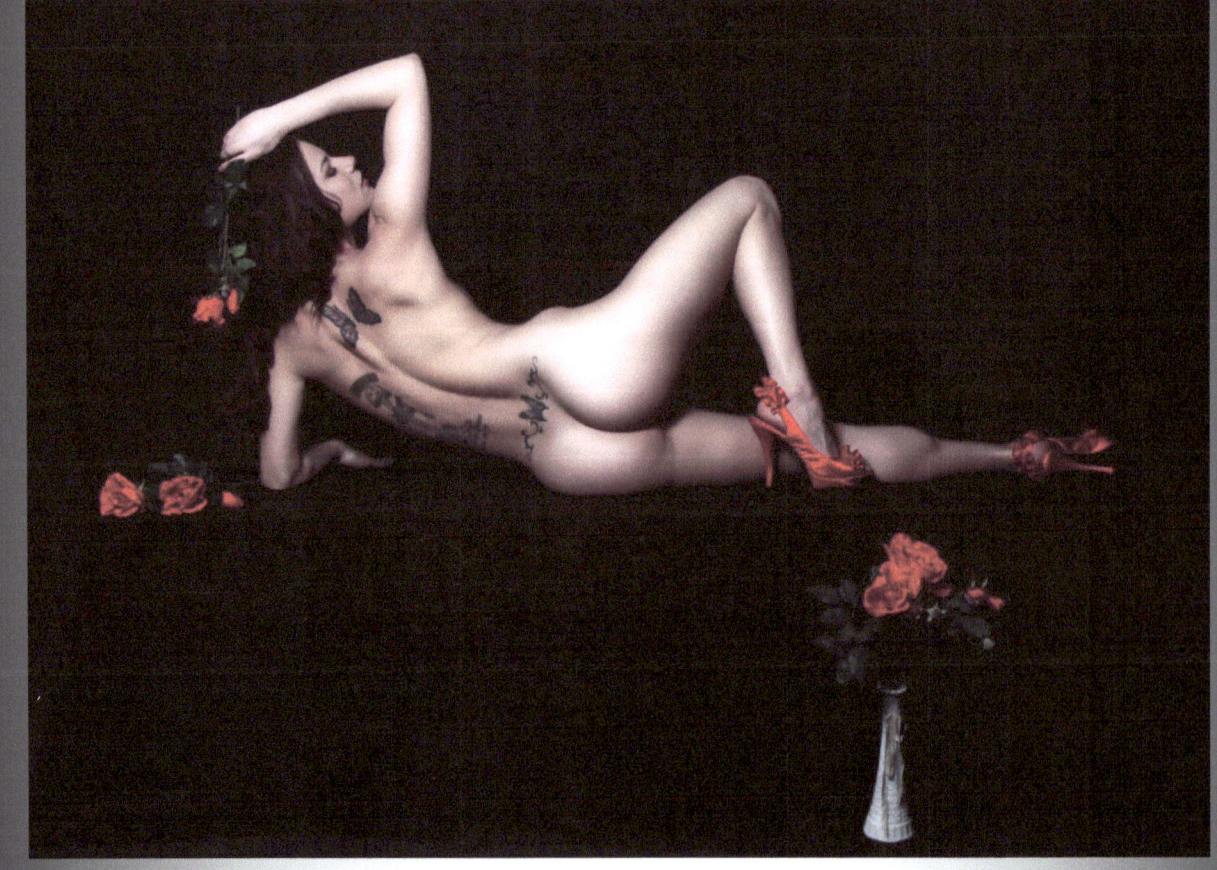

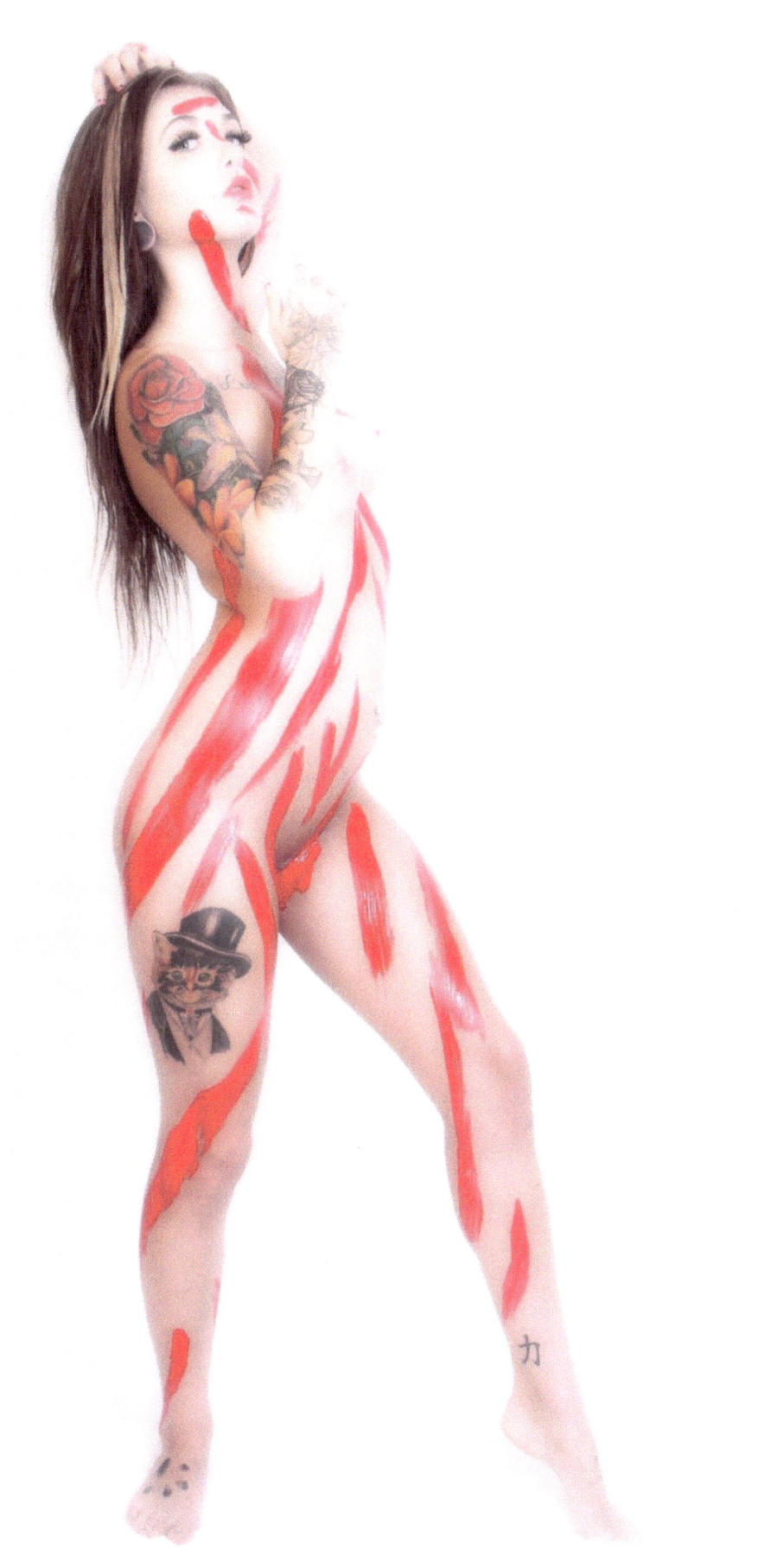

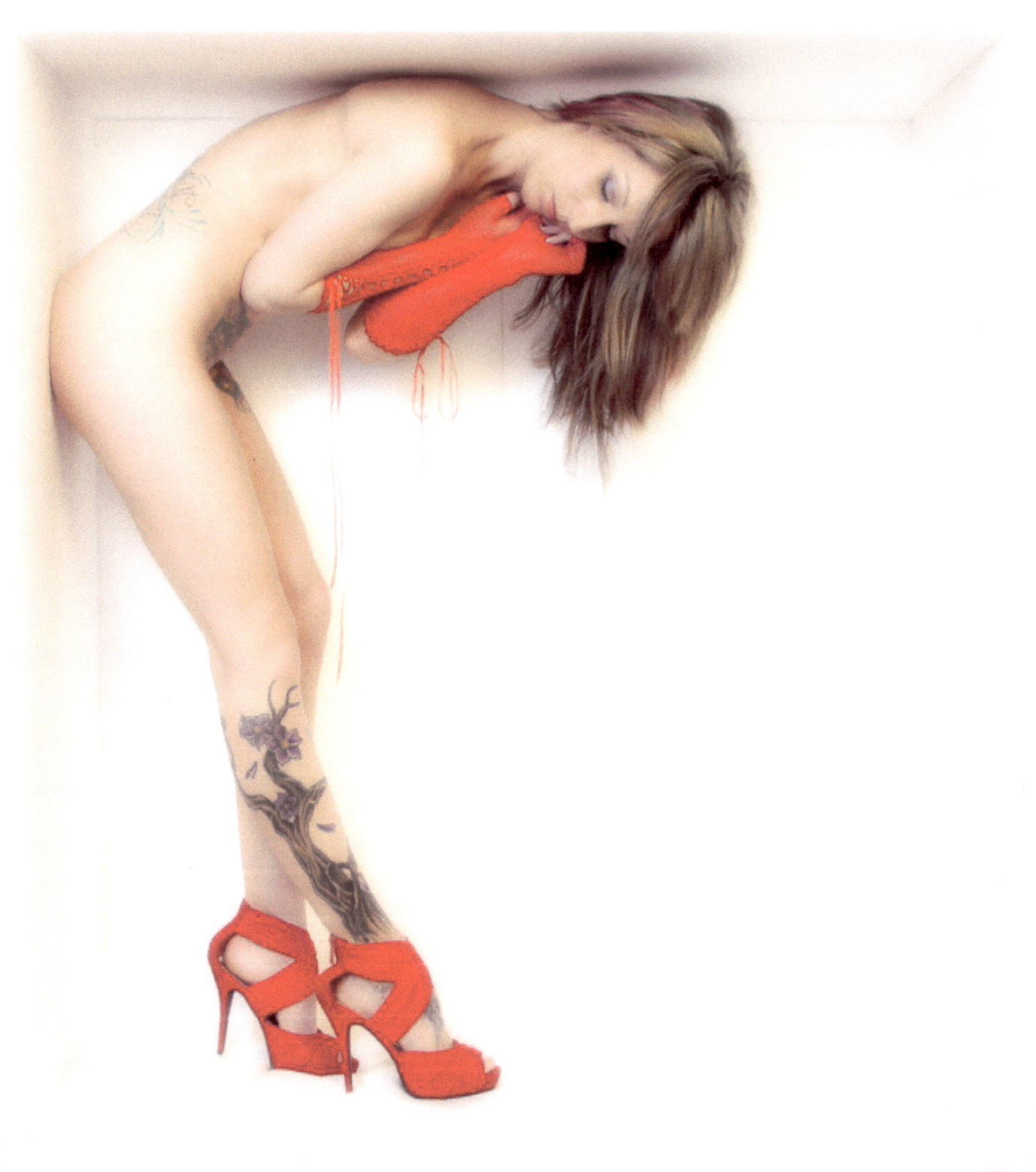

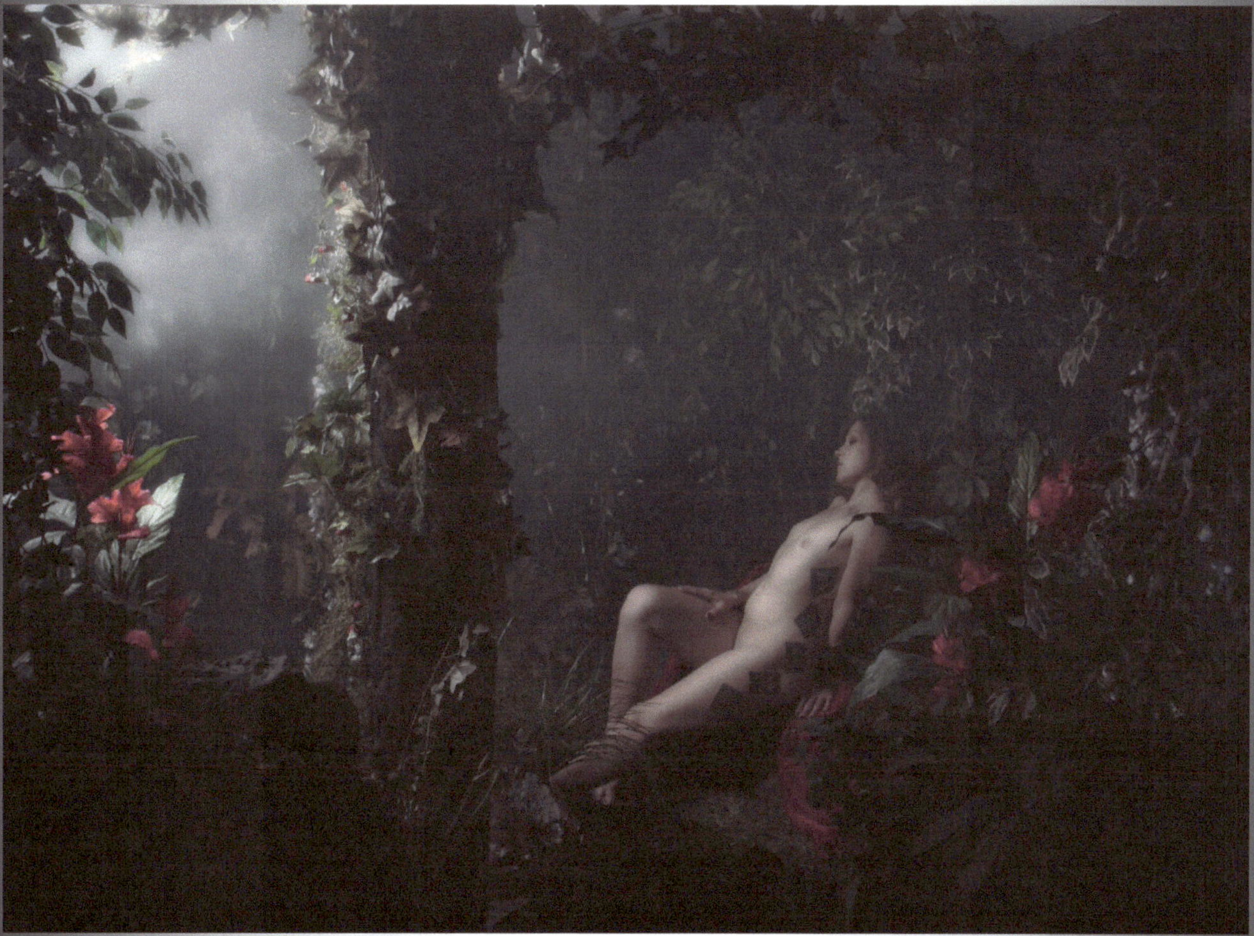
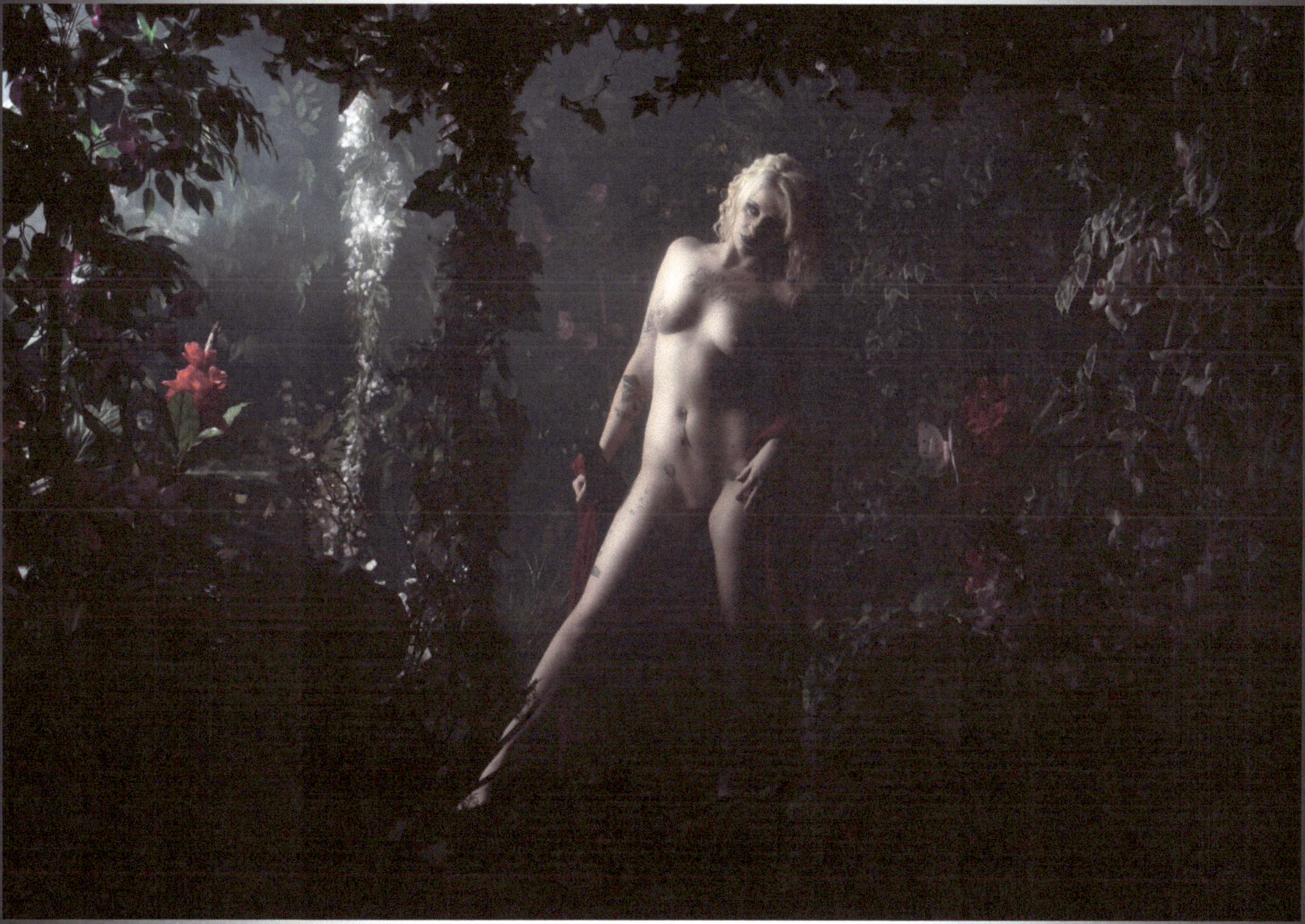

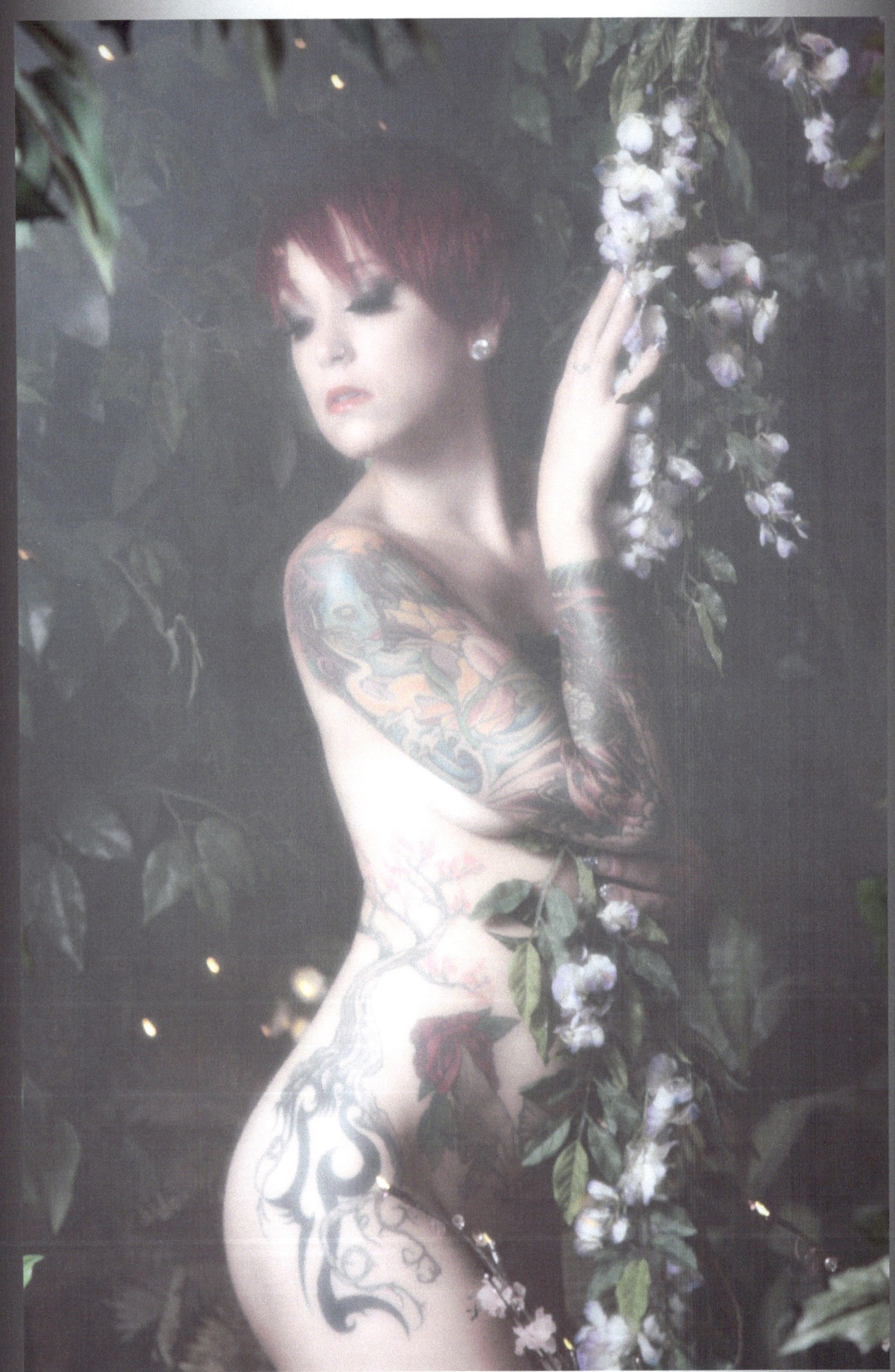

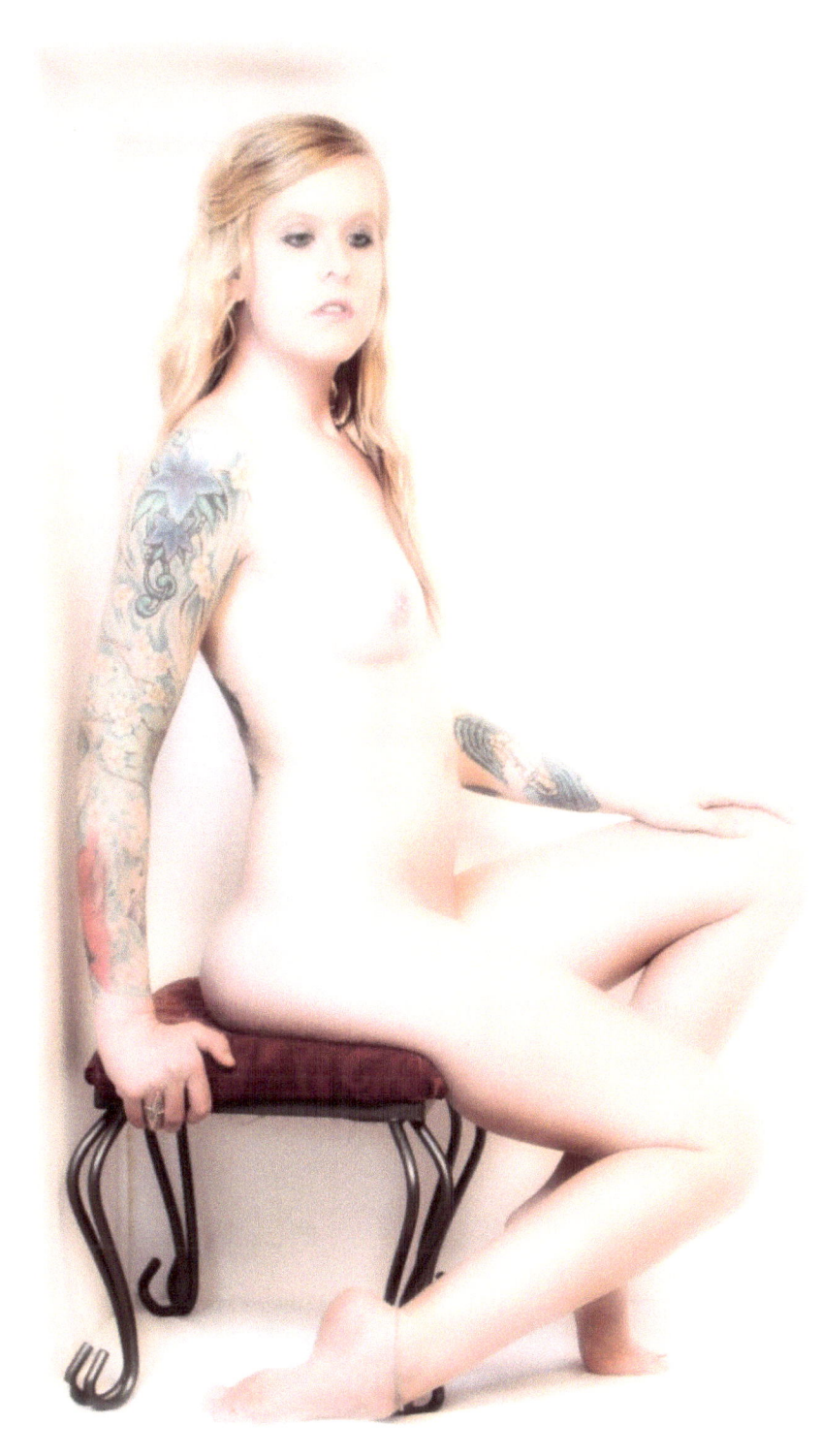

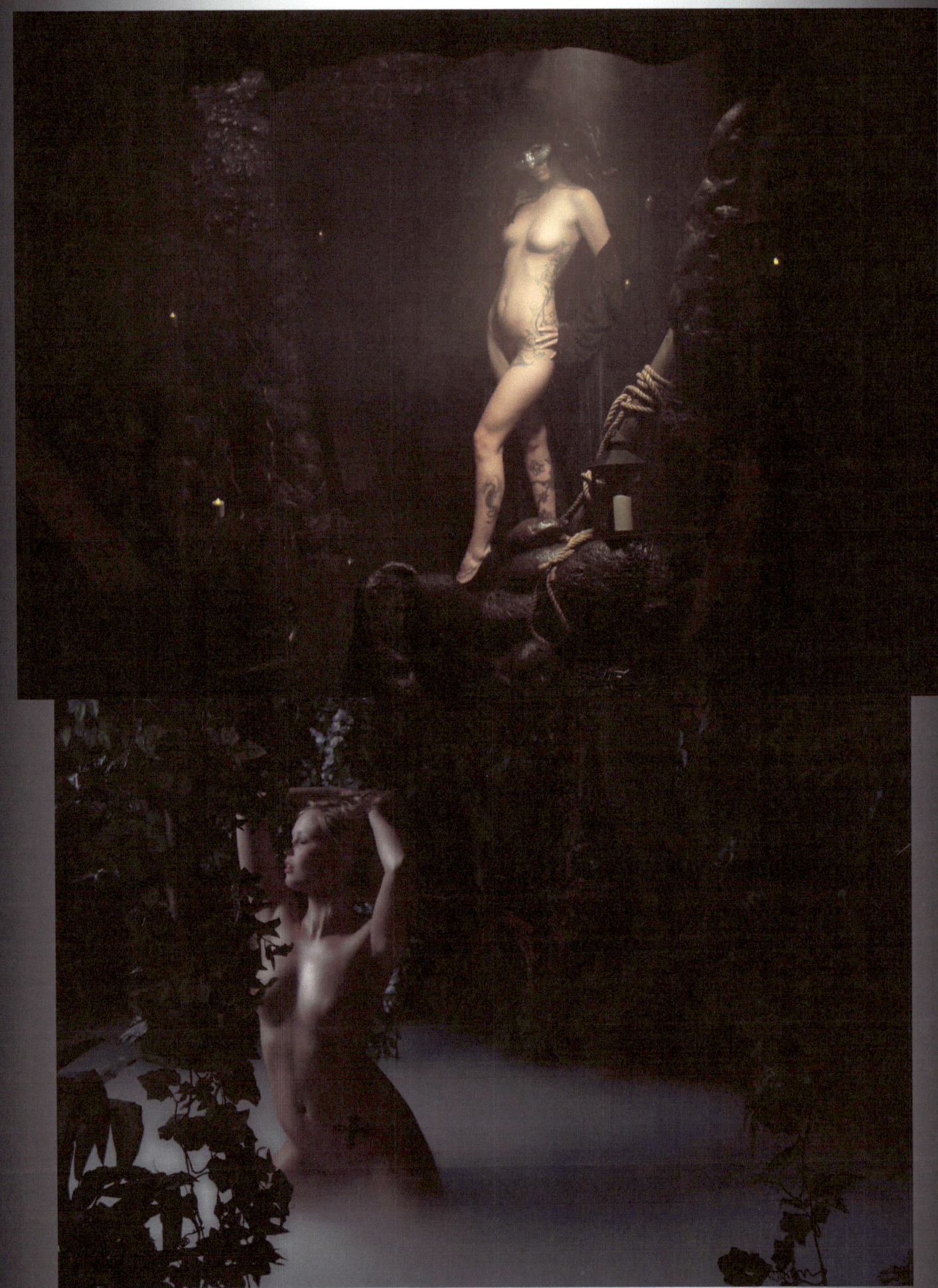

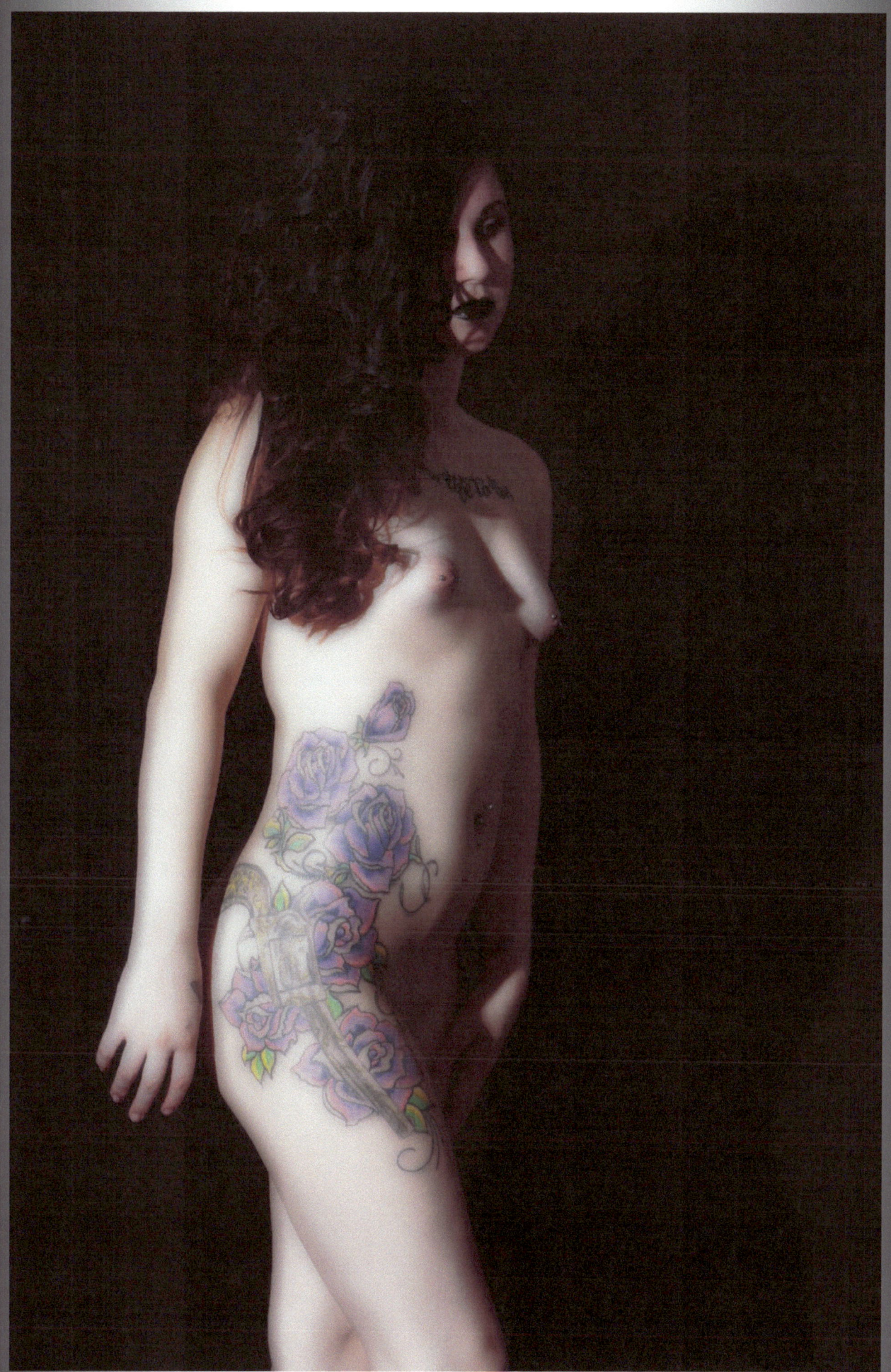

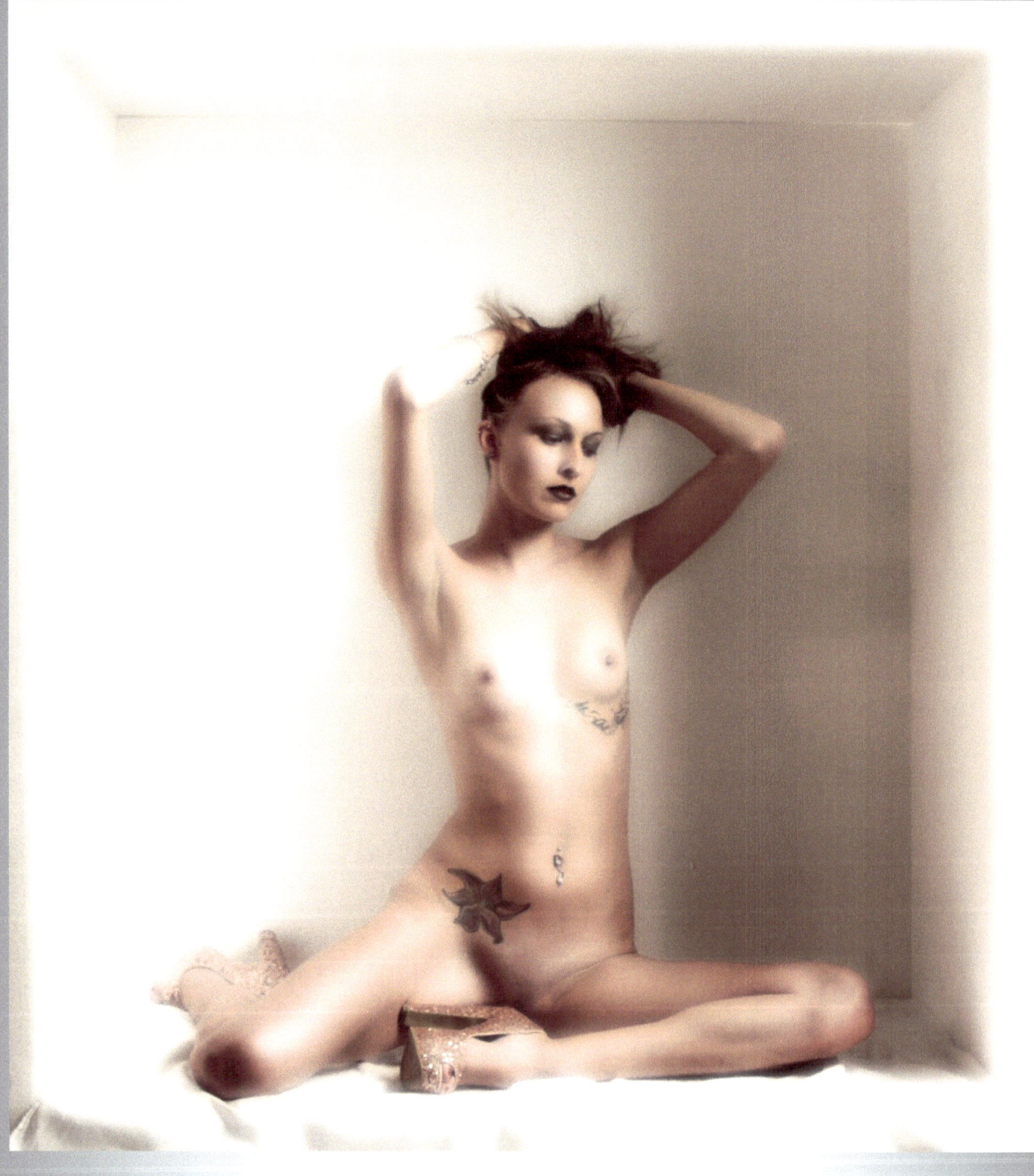

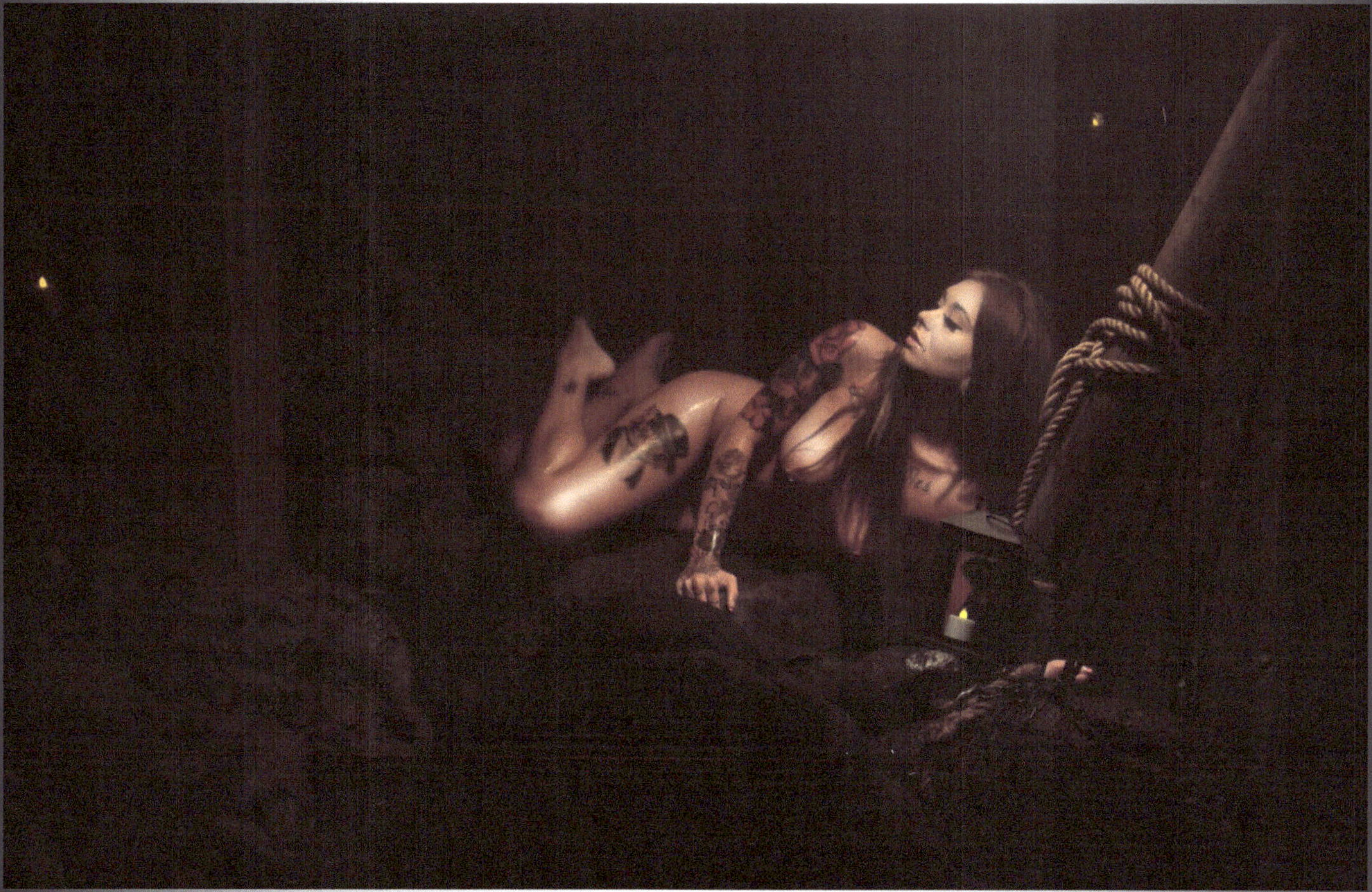

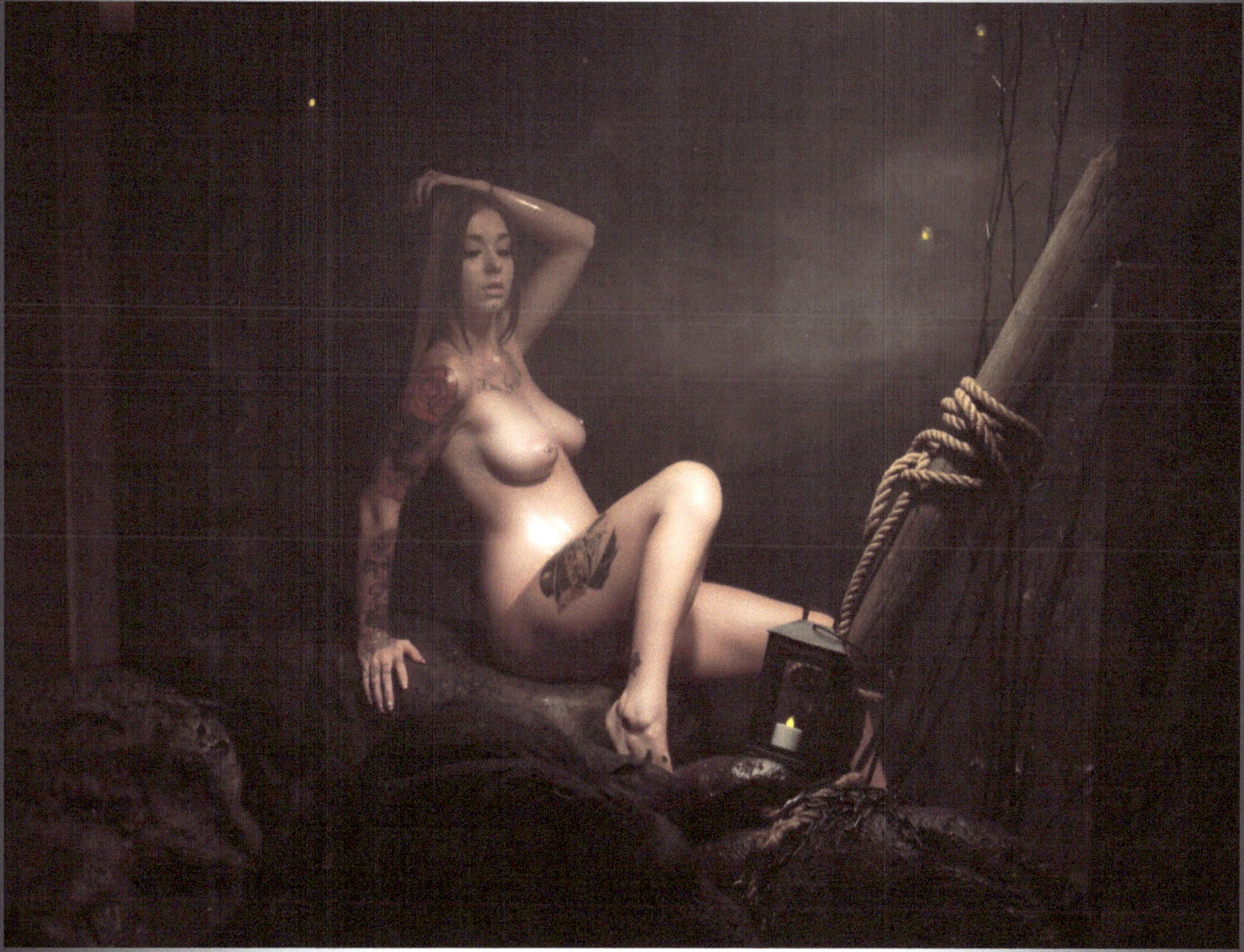

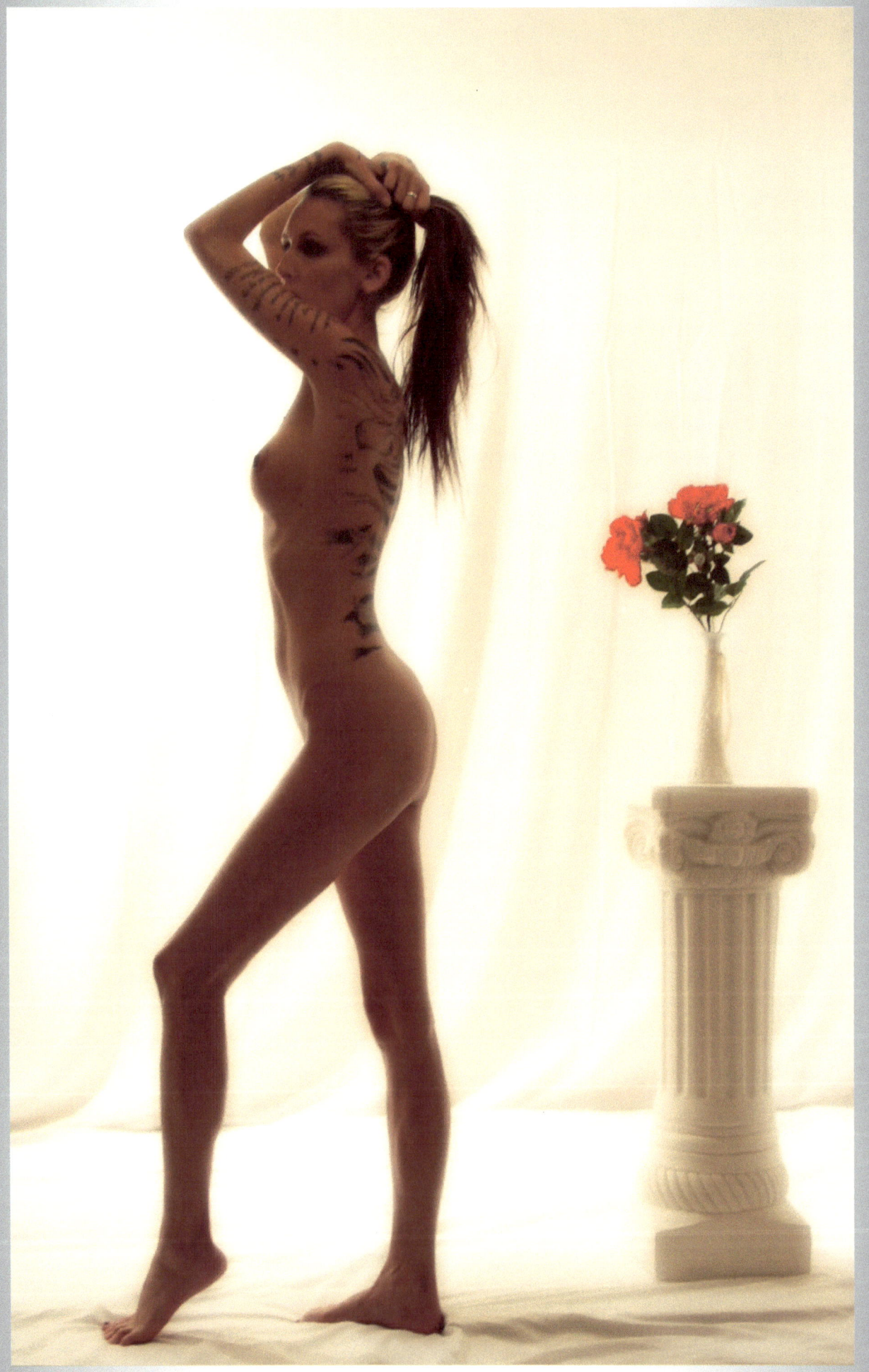

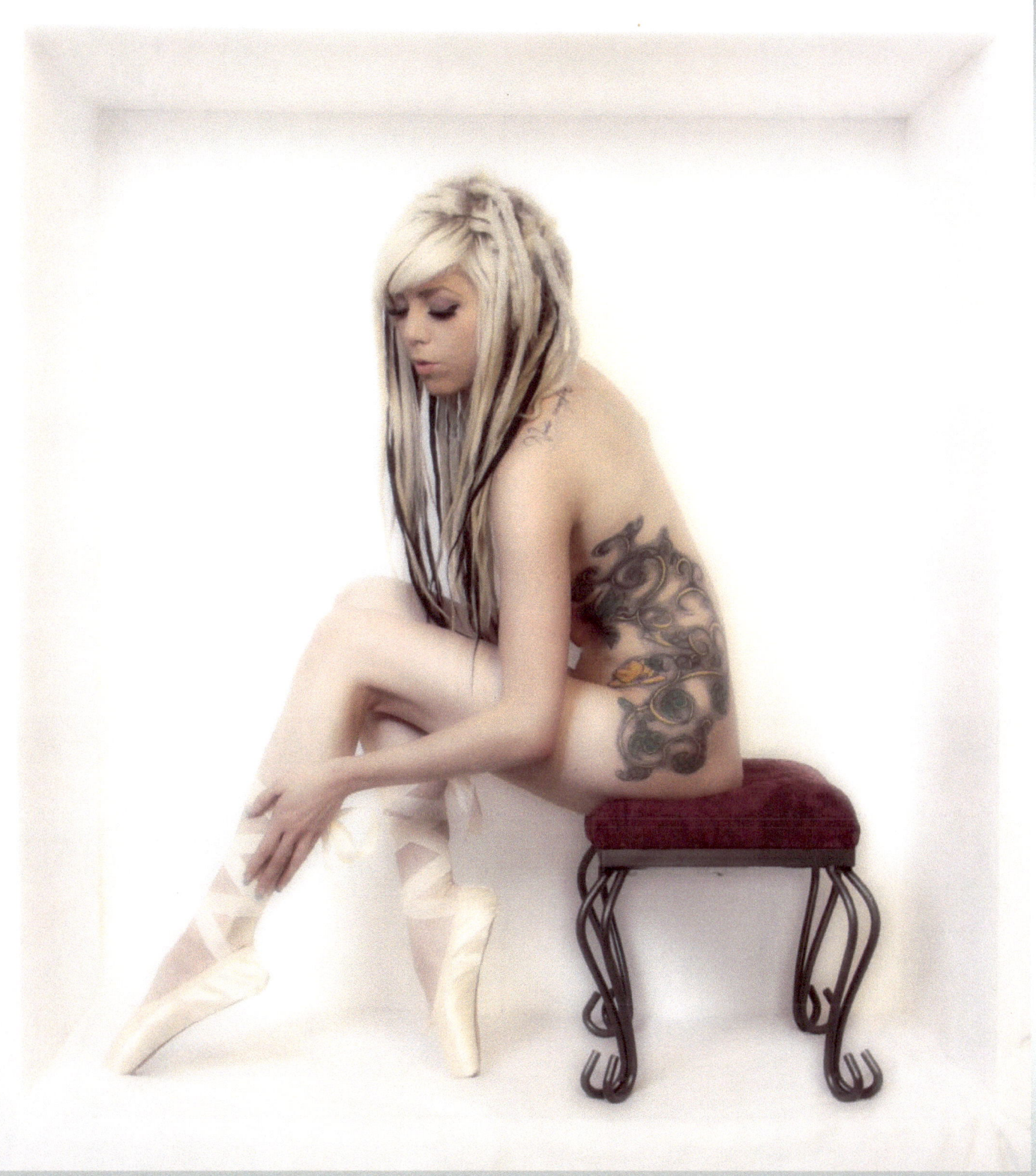

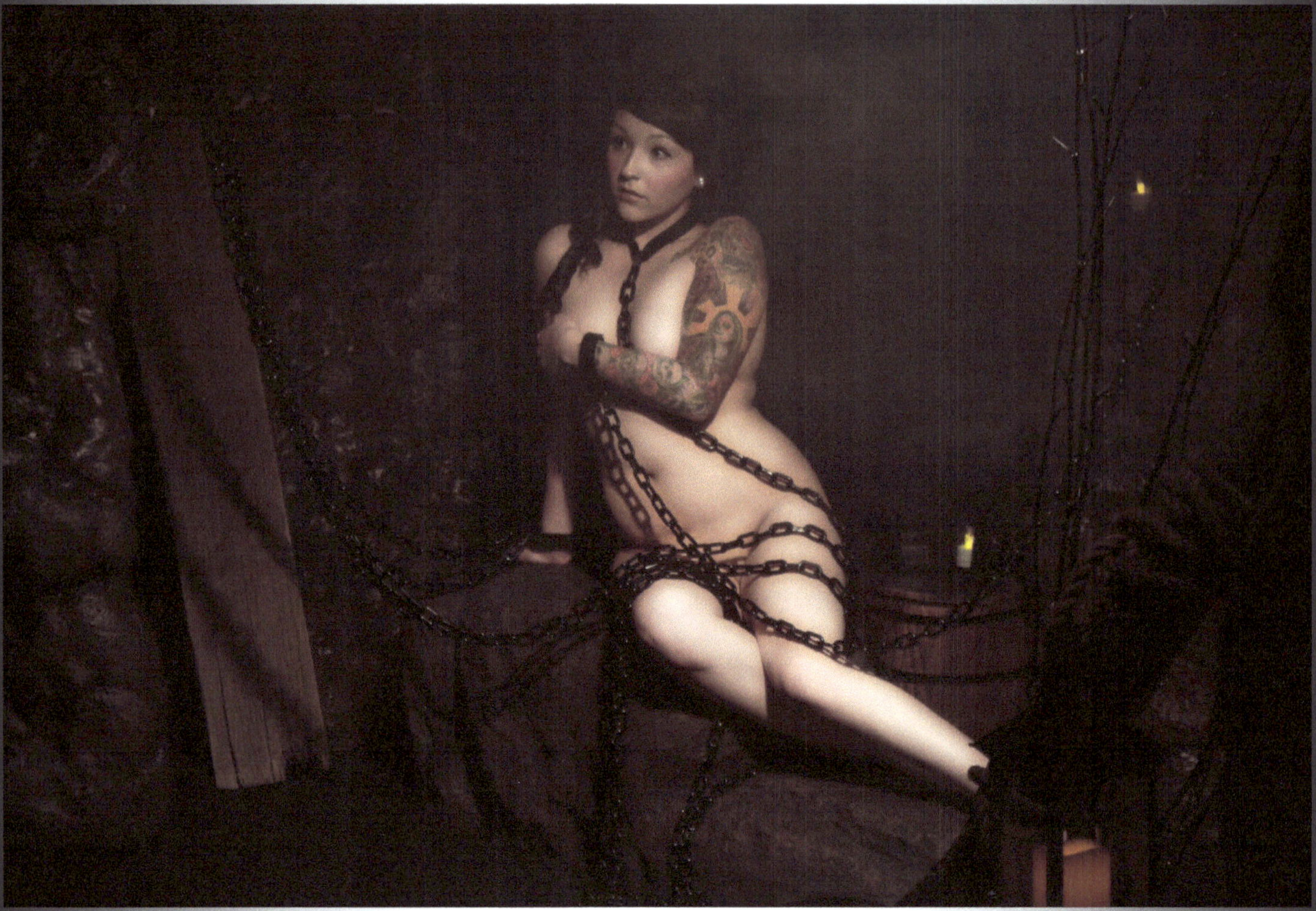

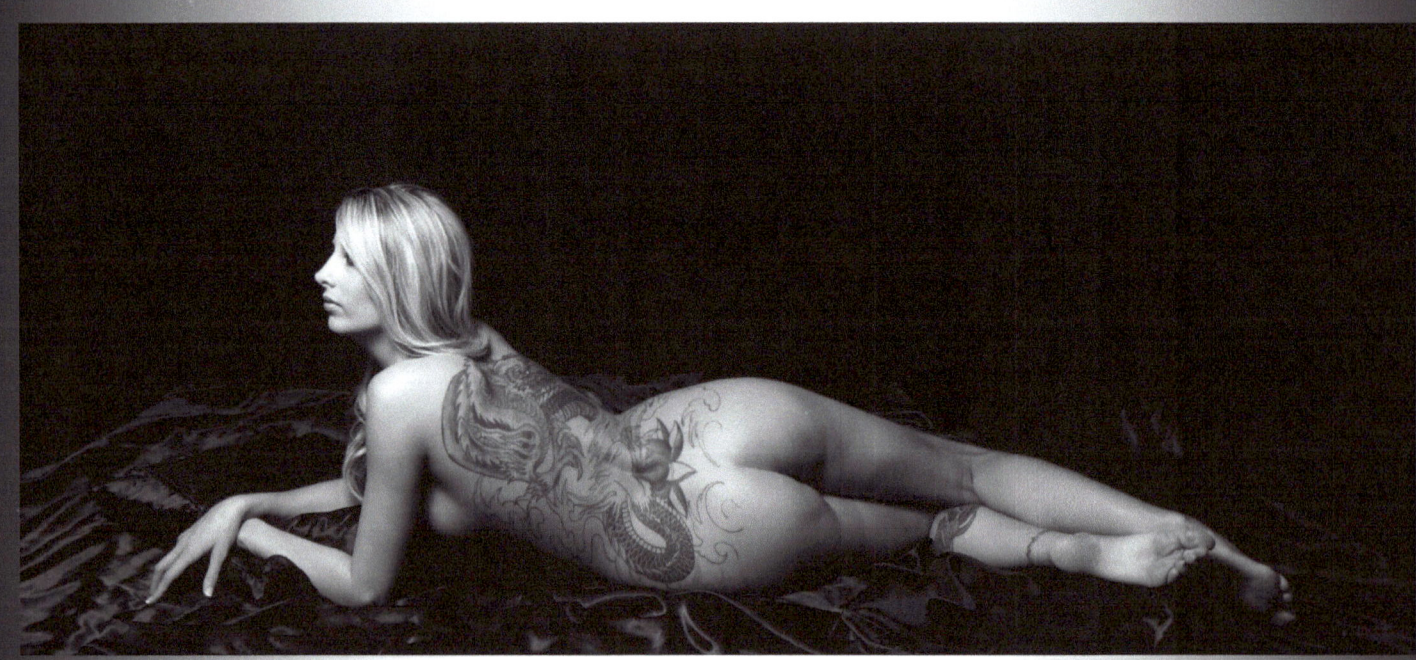

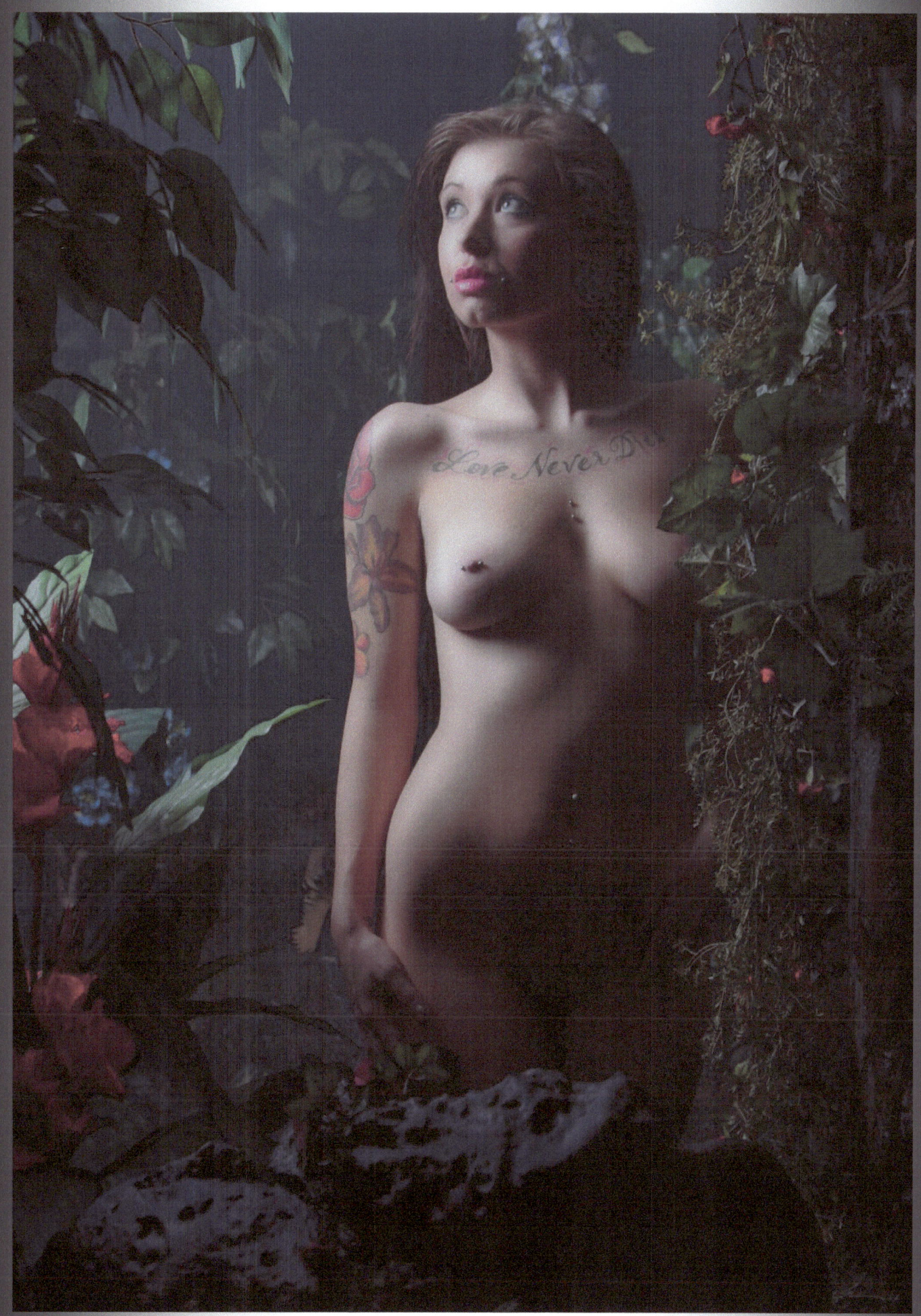

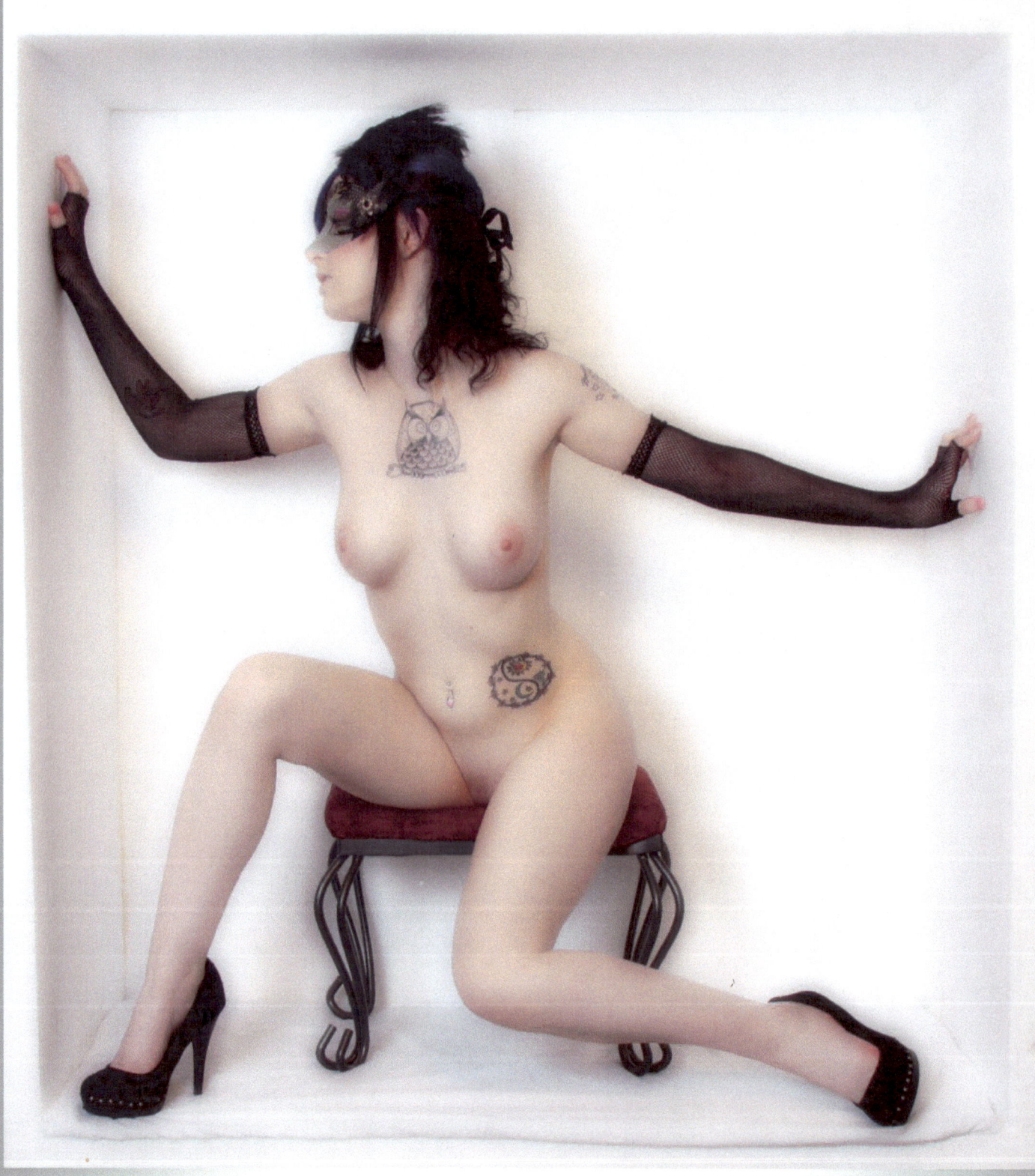

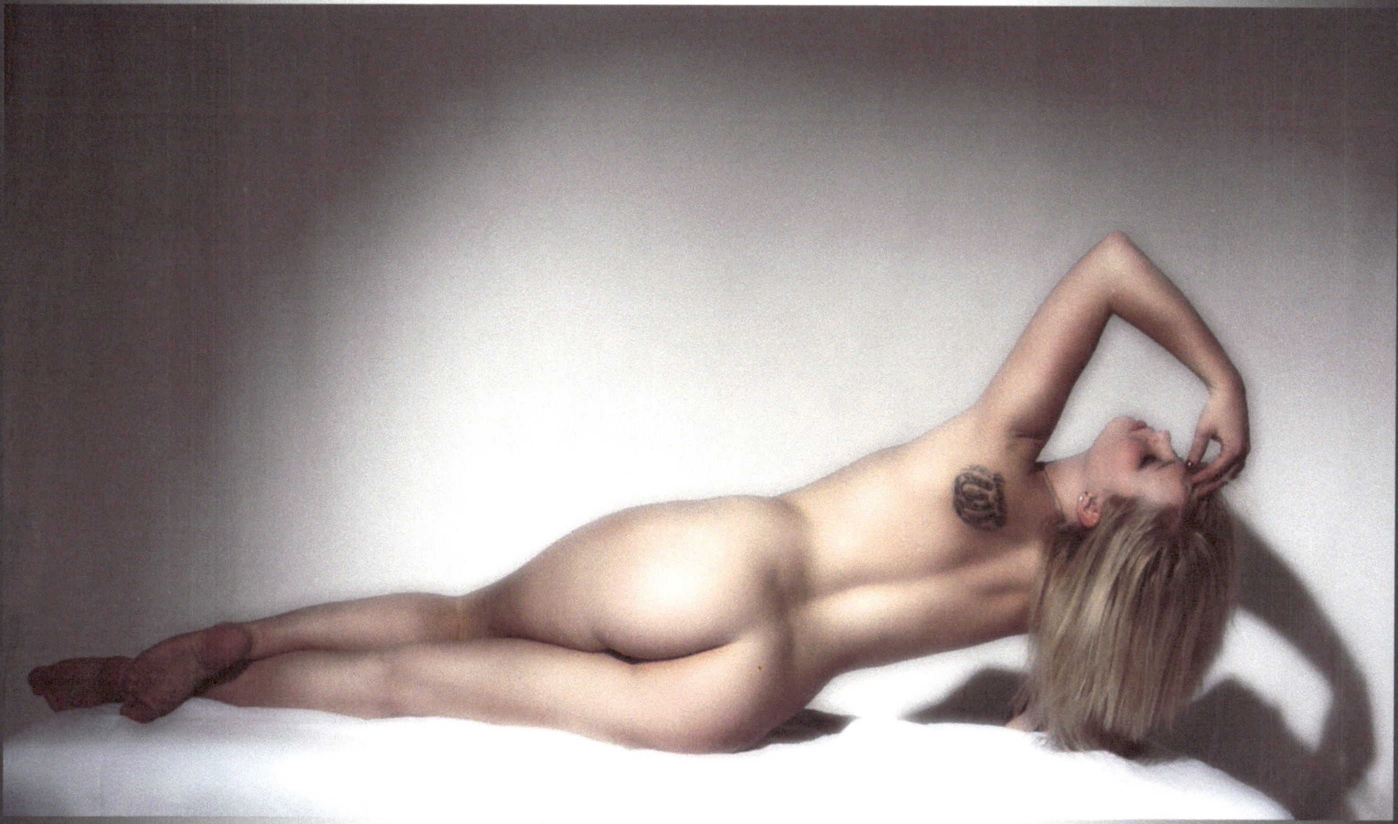

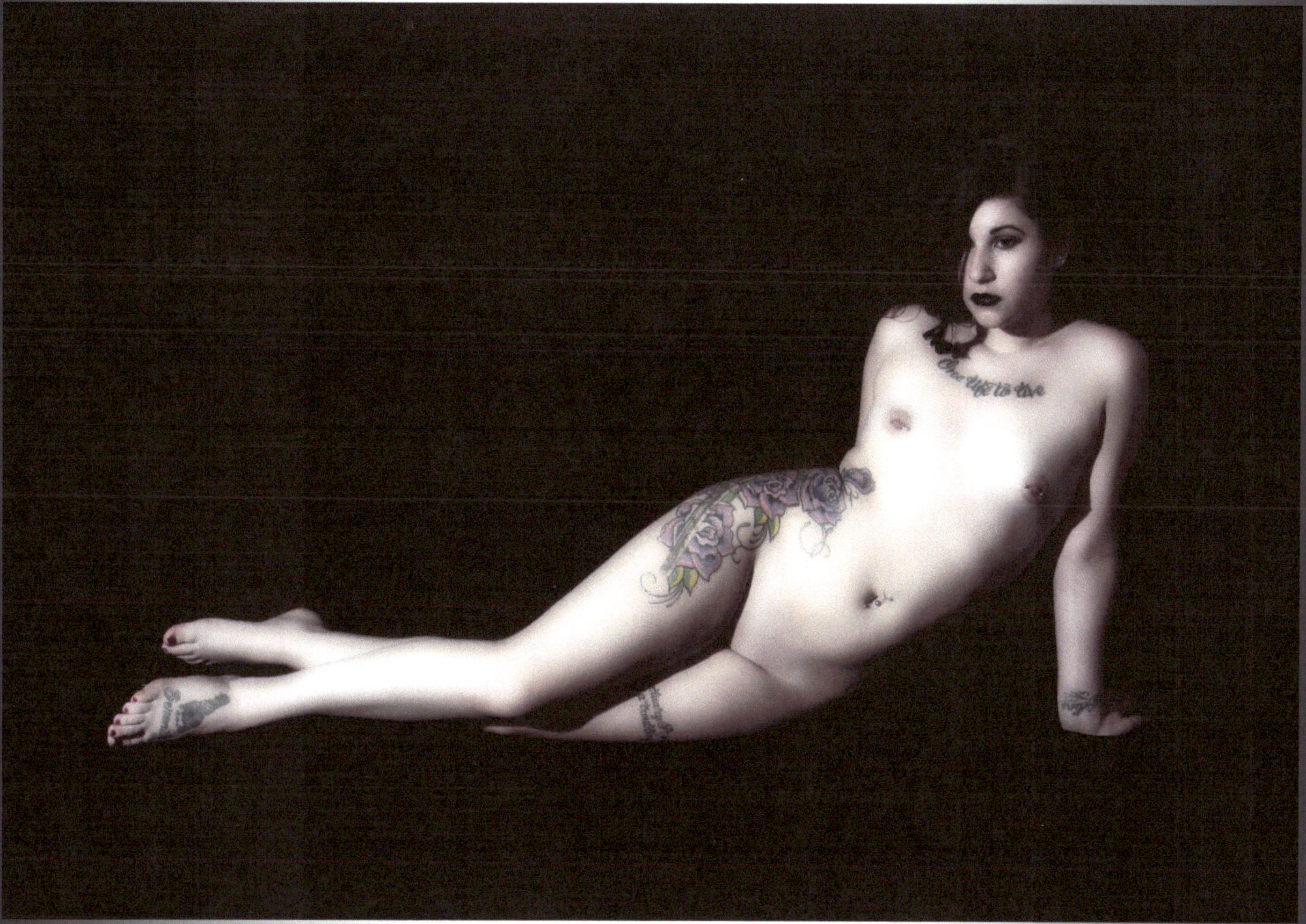

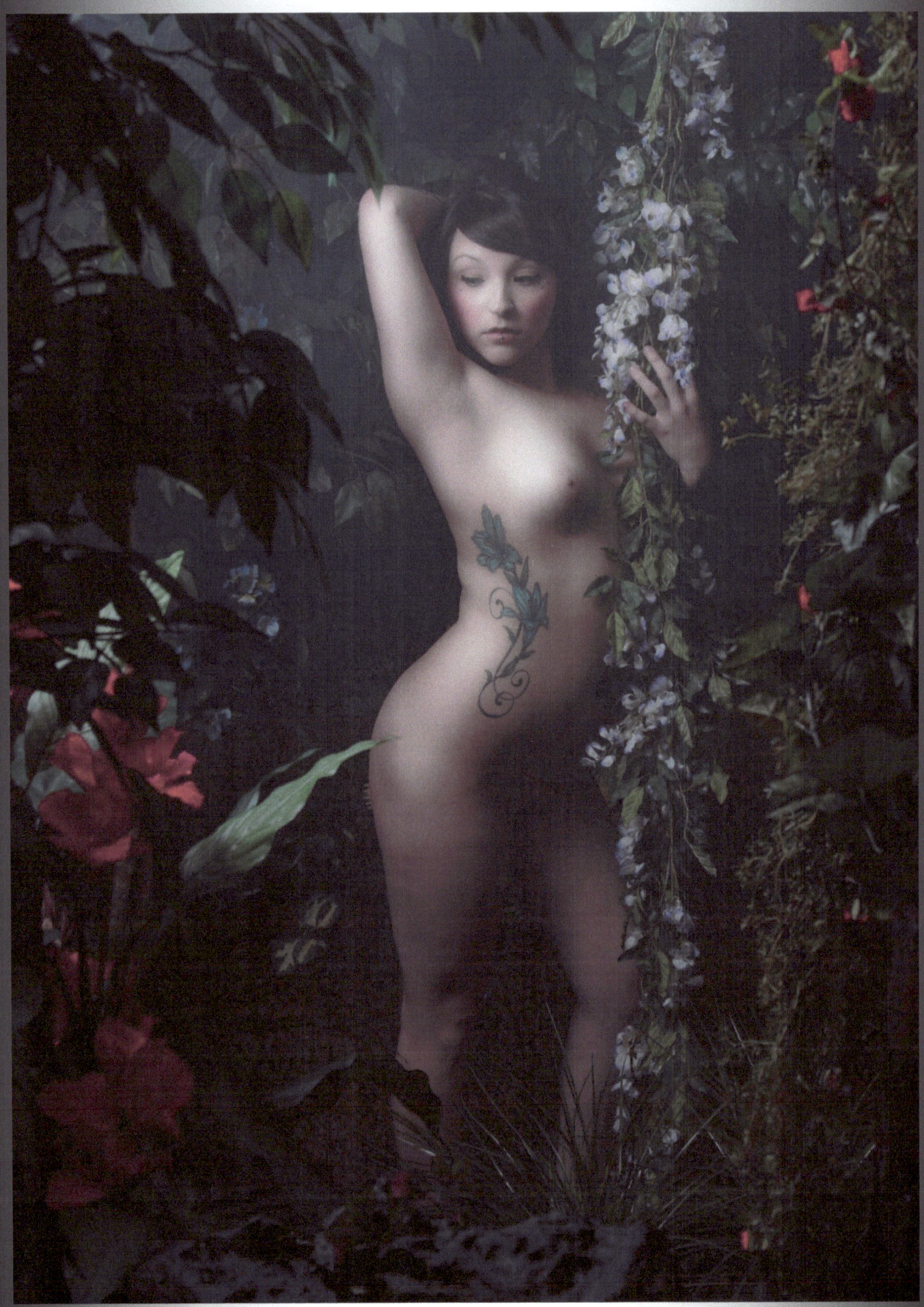

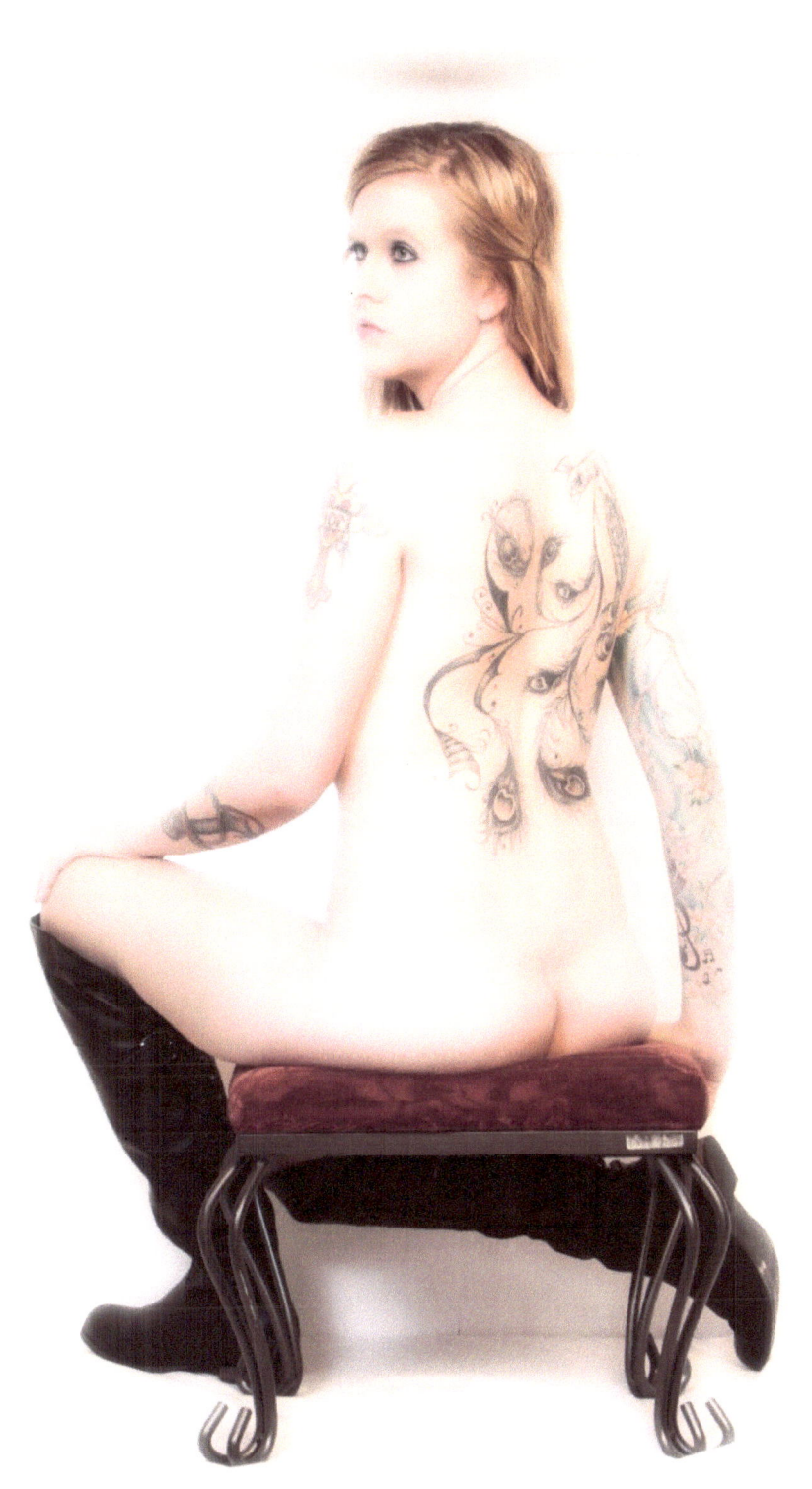

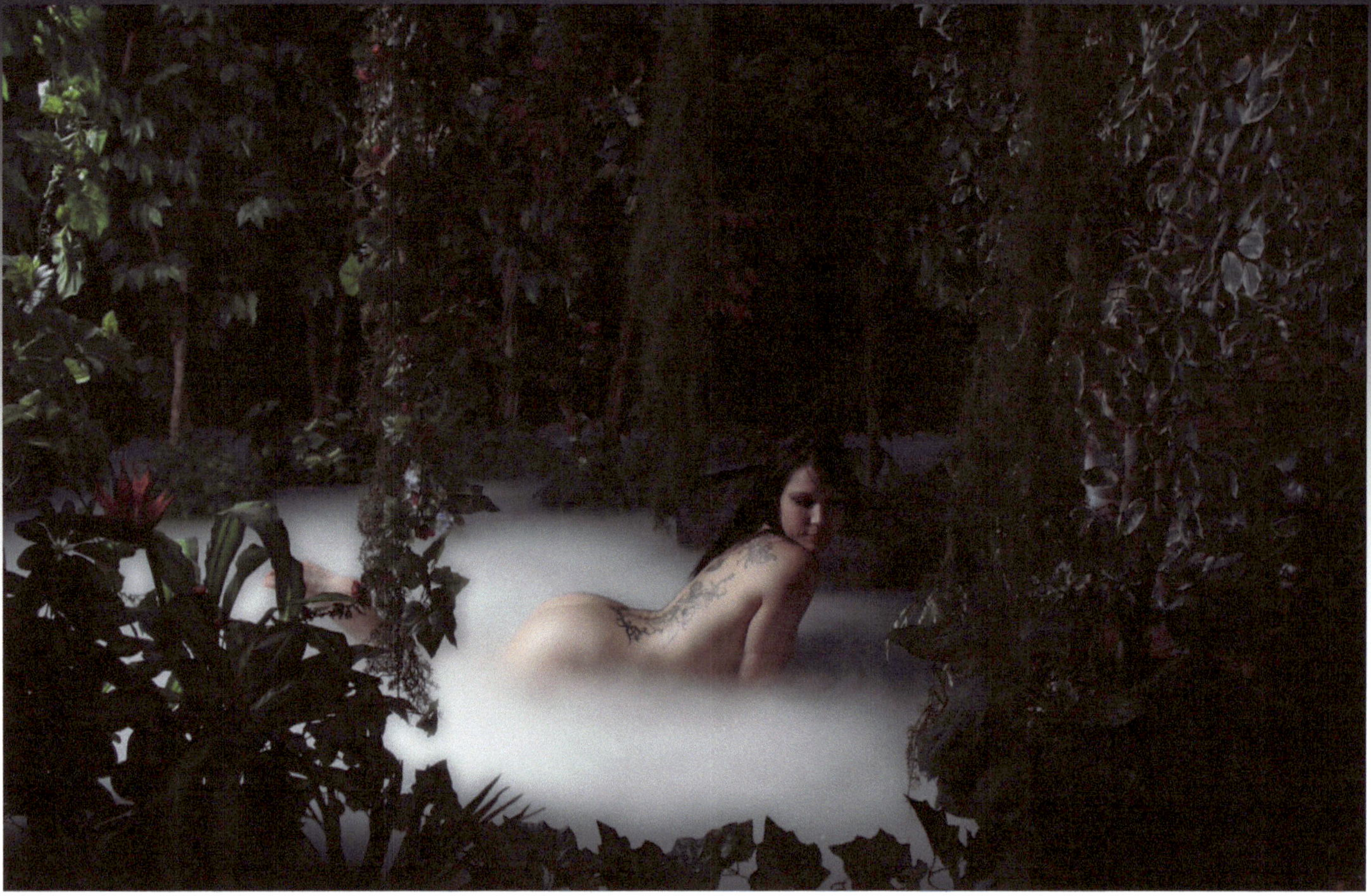

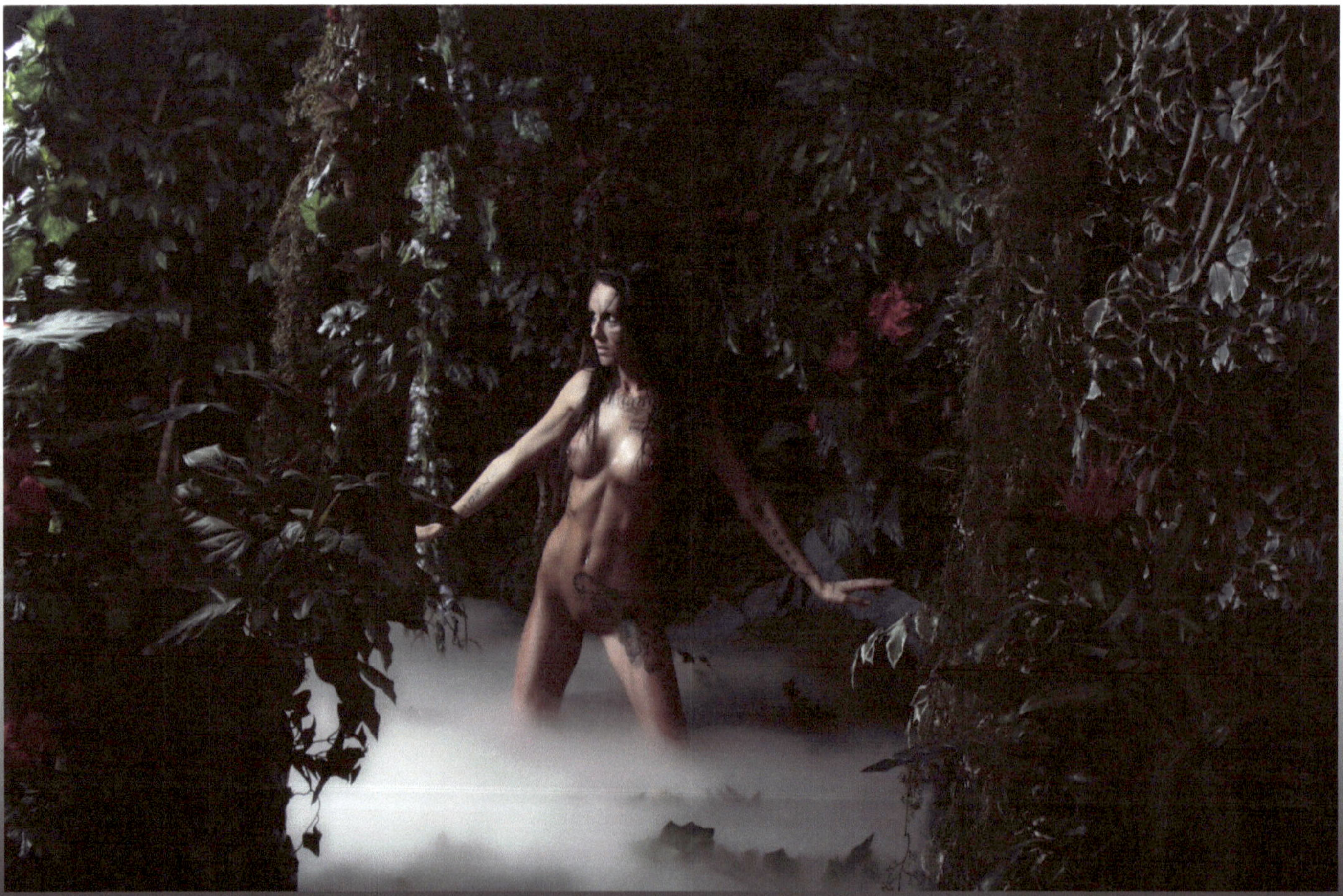

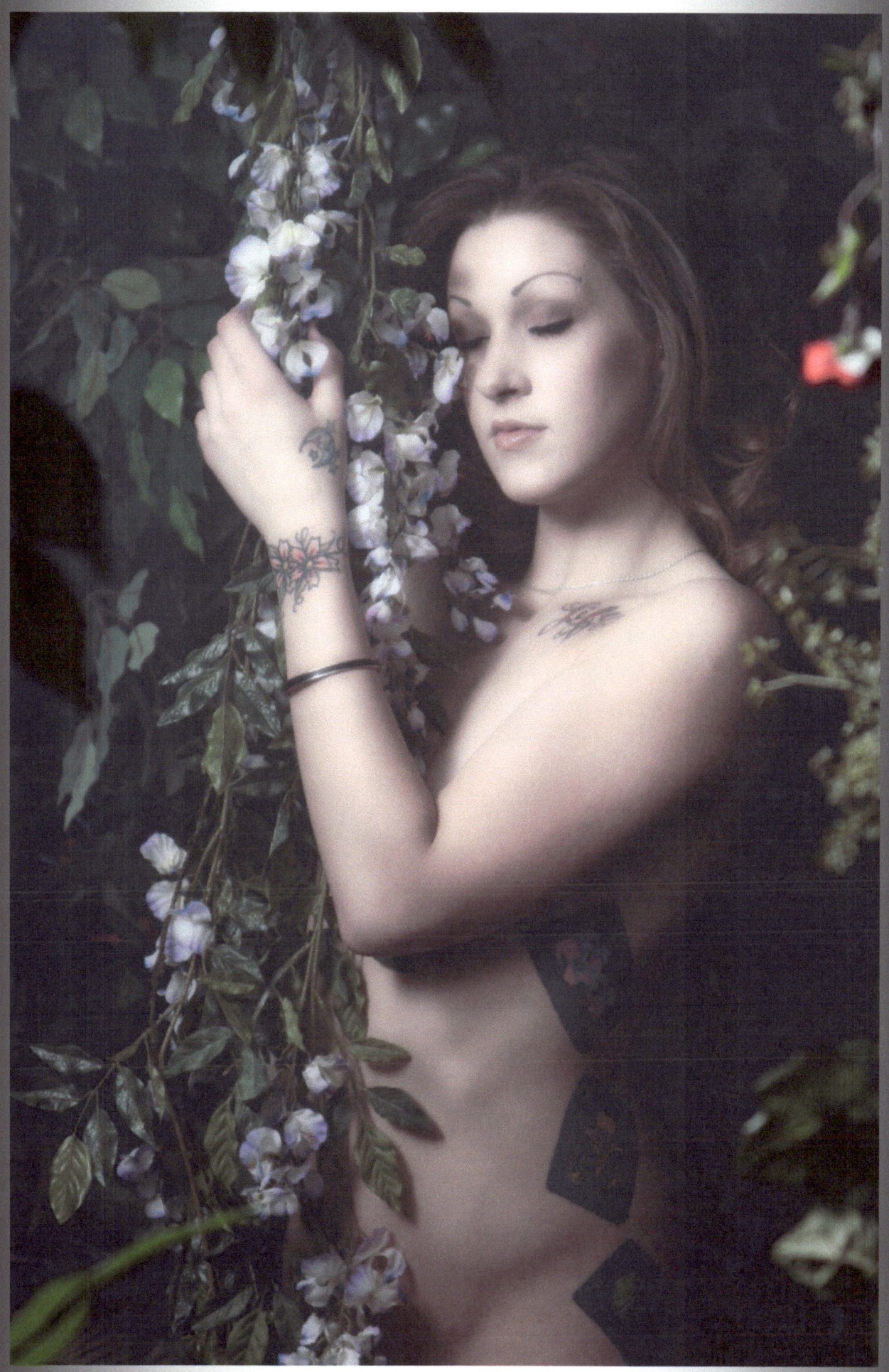

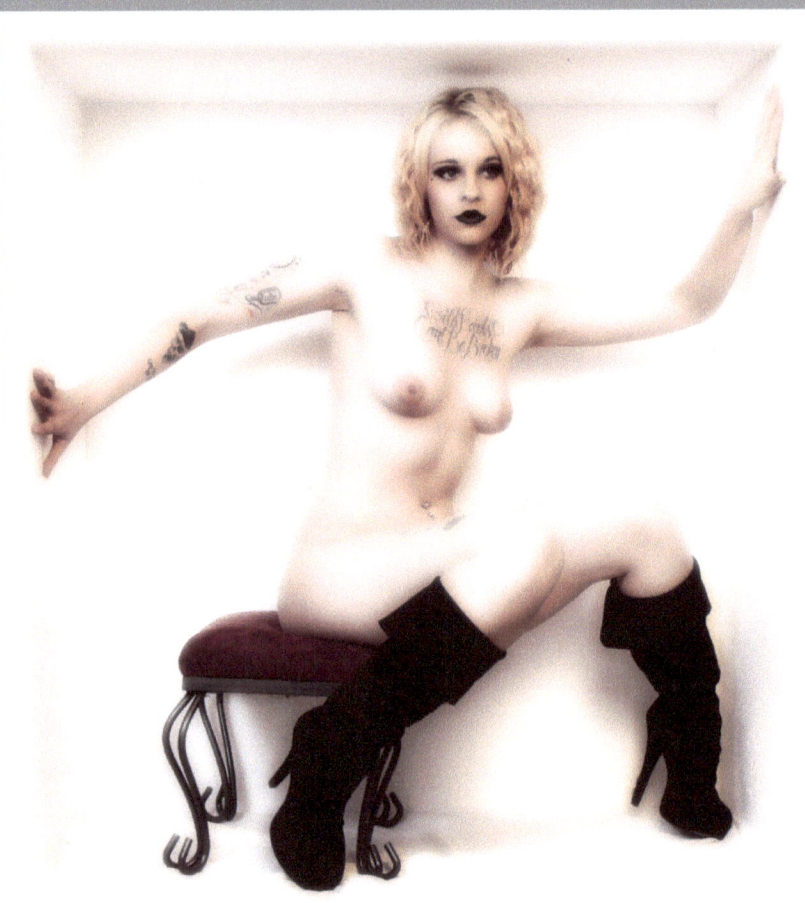
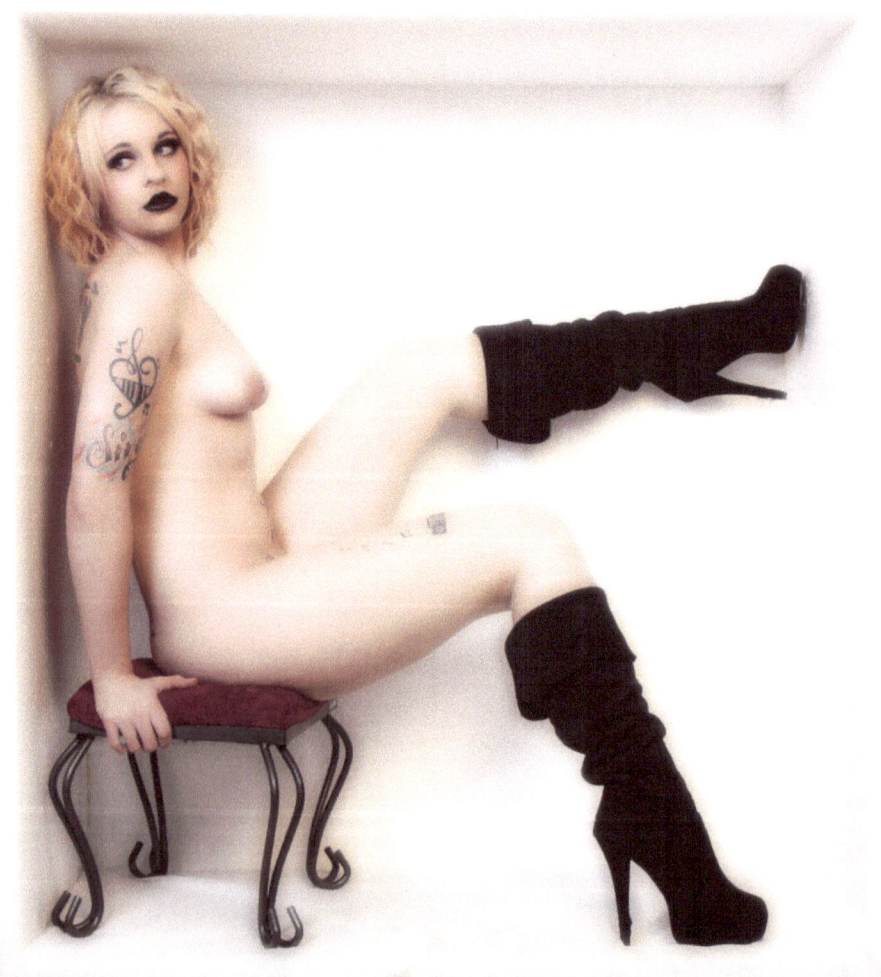

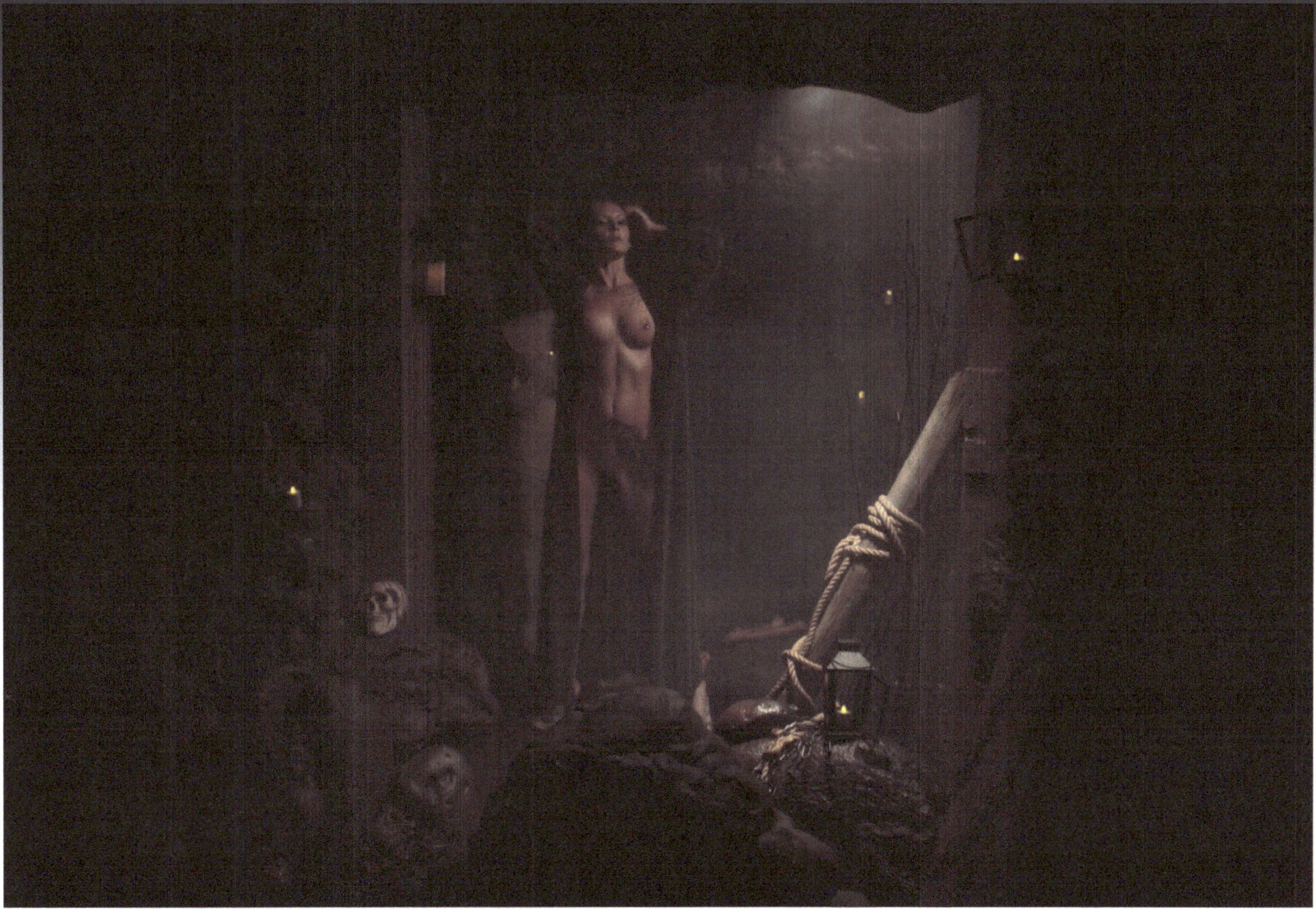

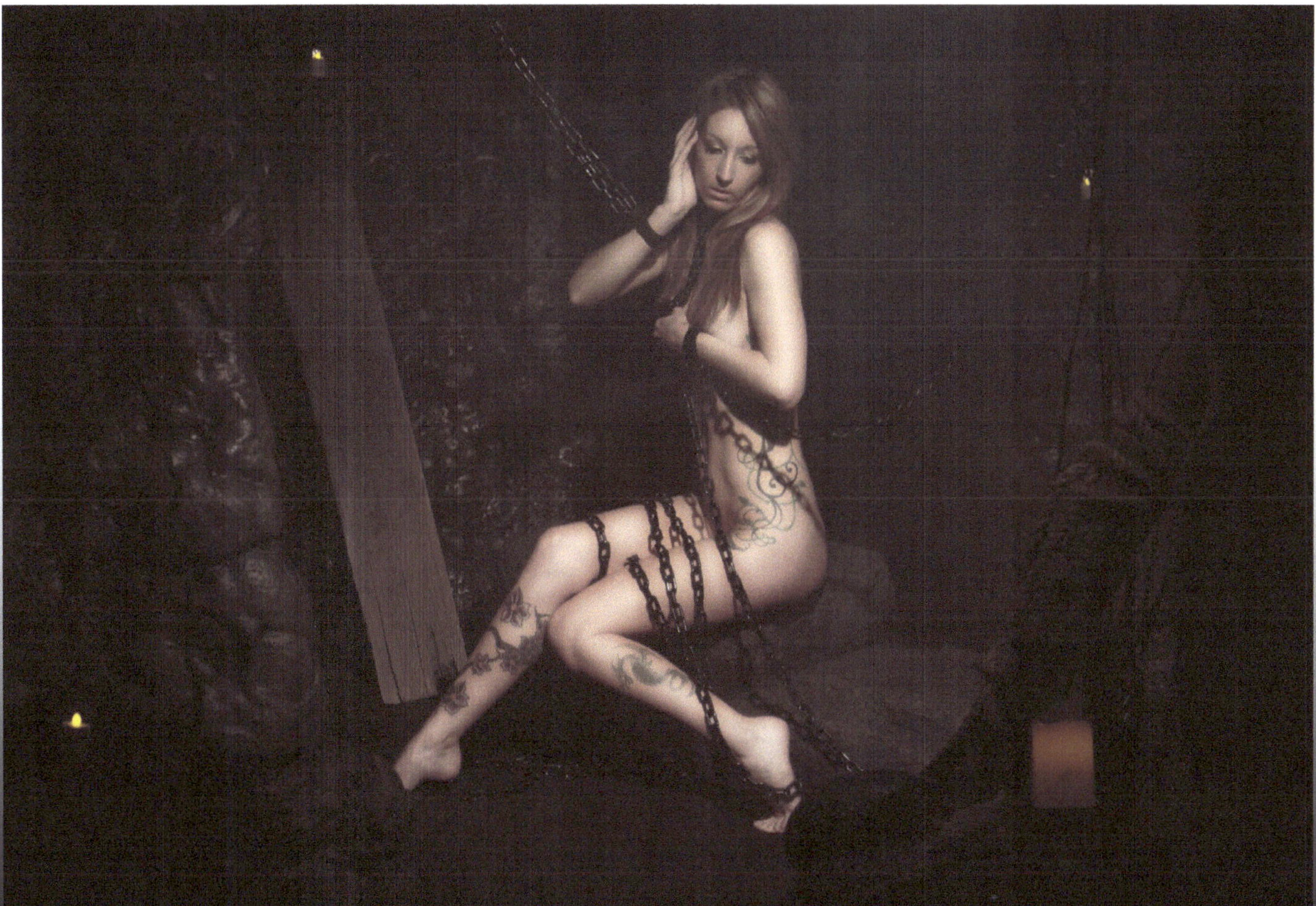

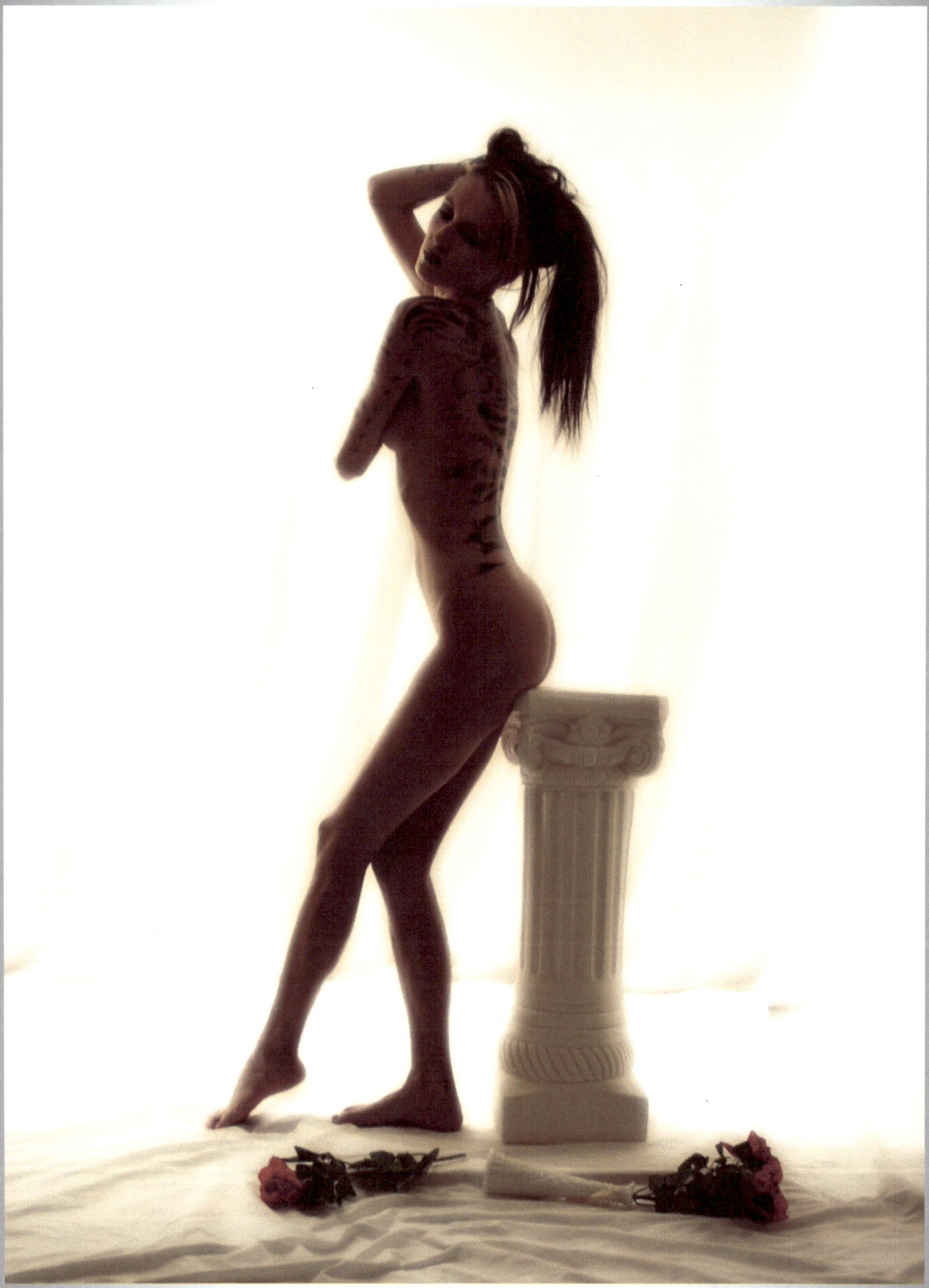

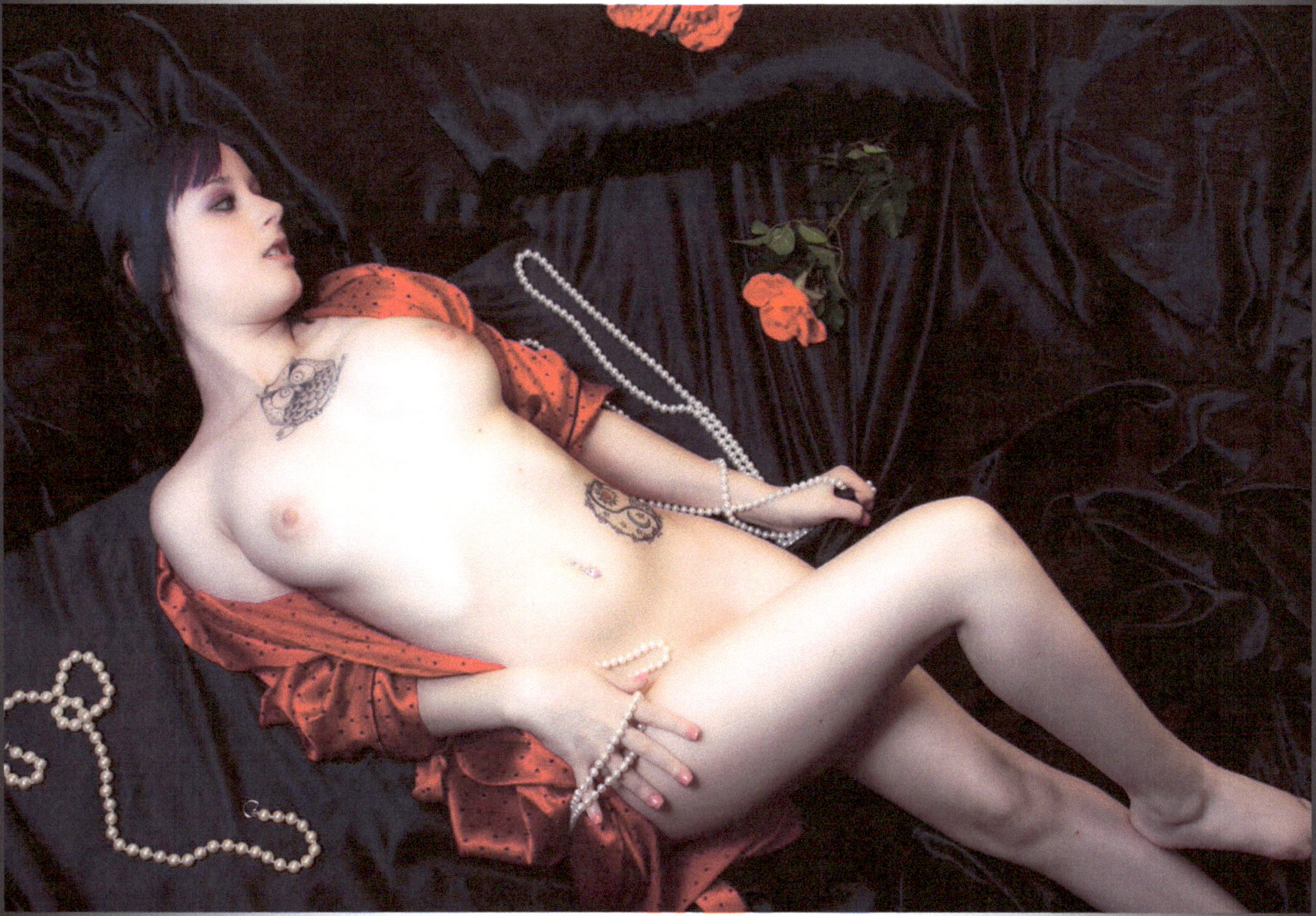

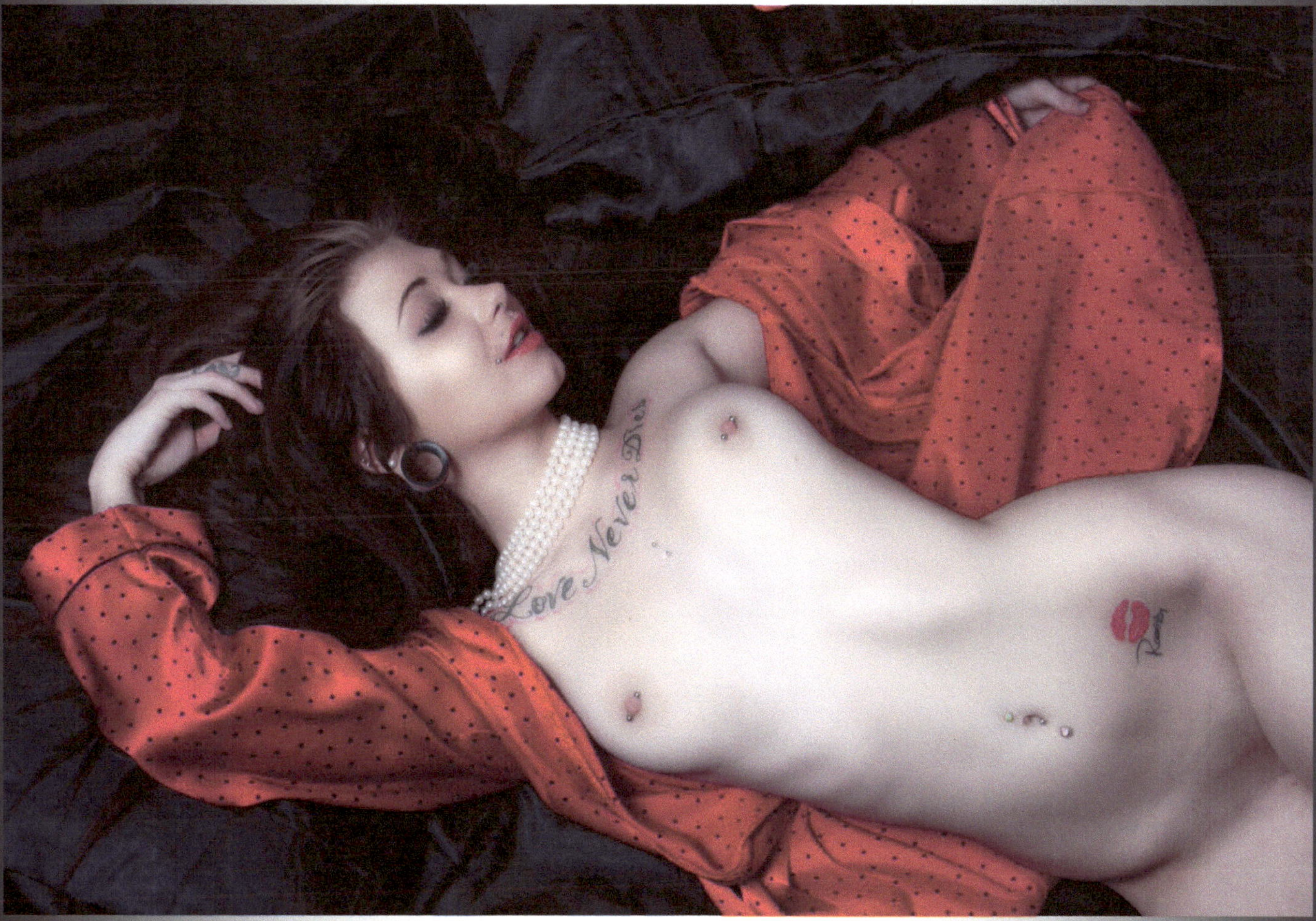
Love Never Dies

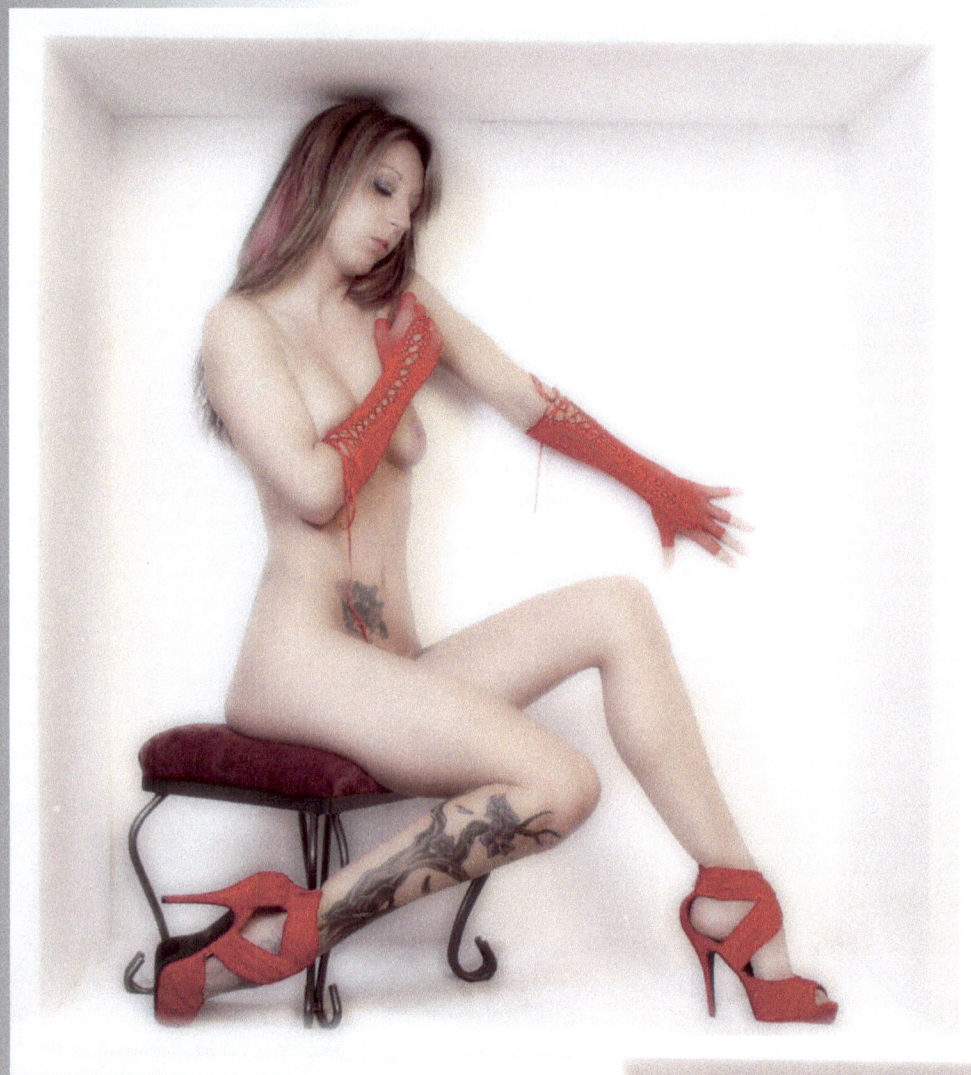
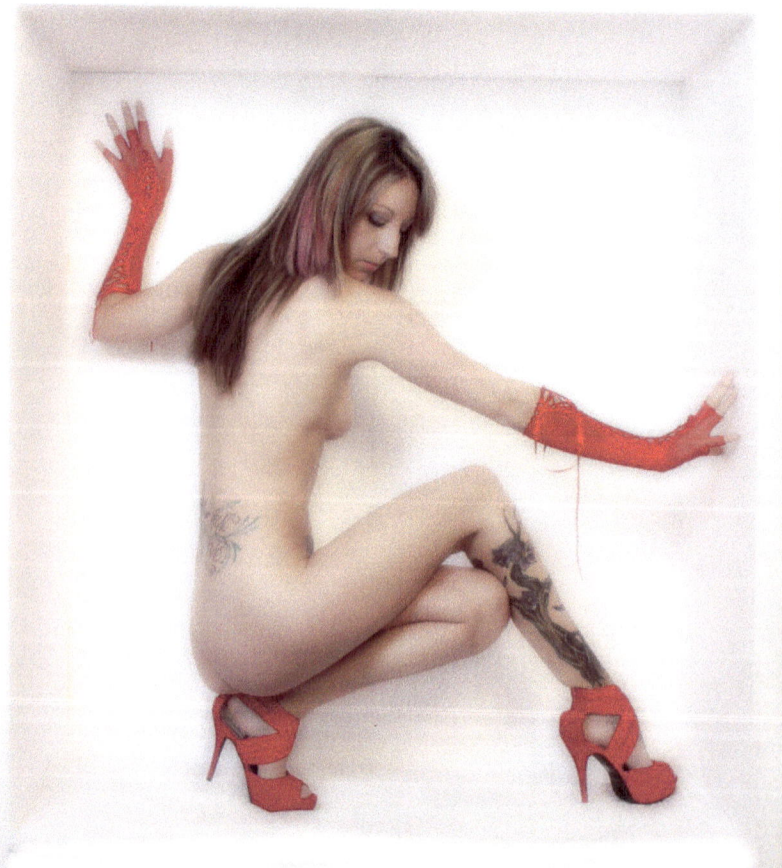

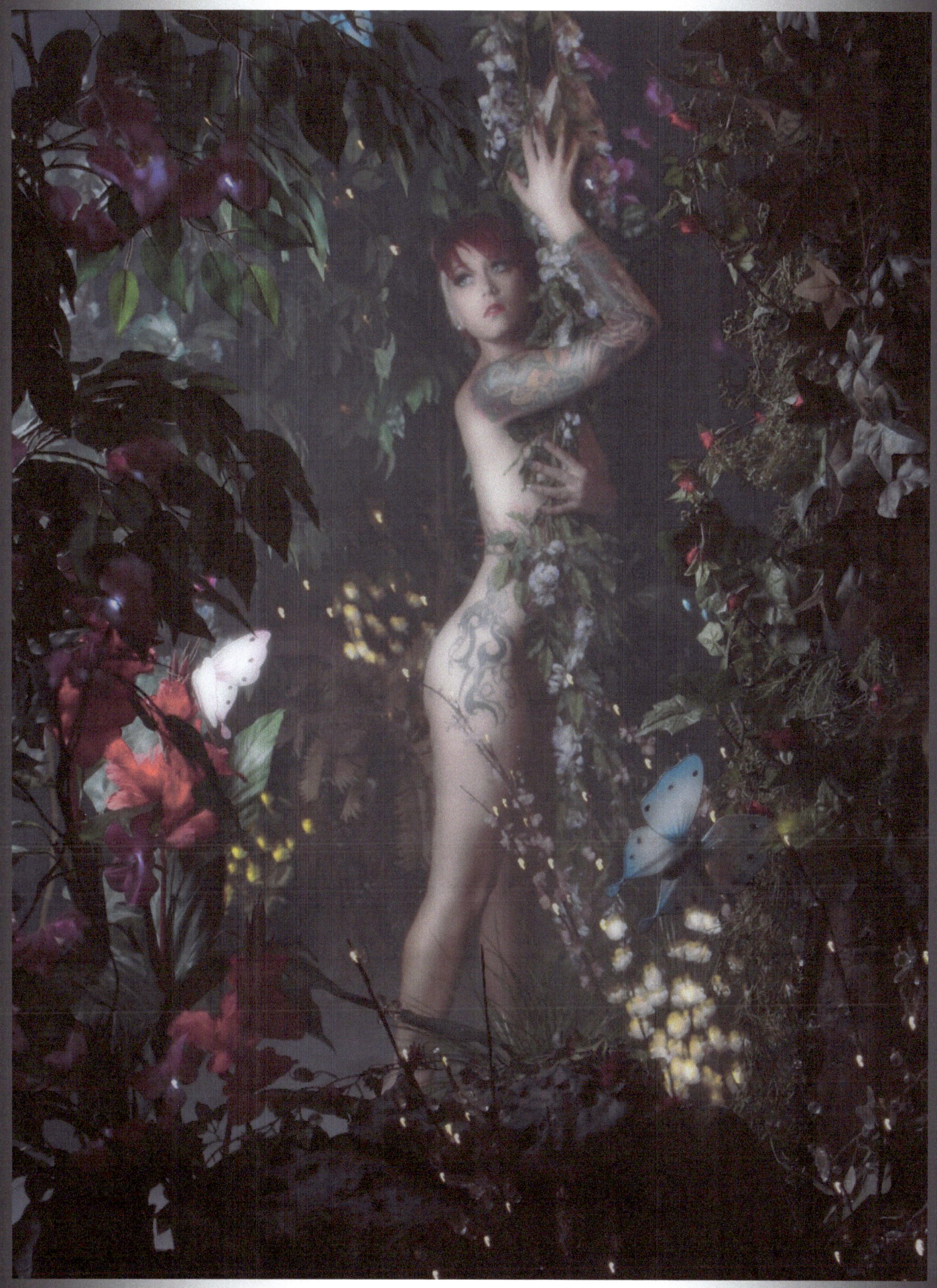

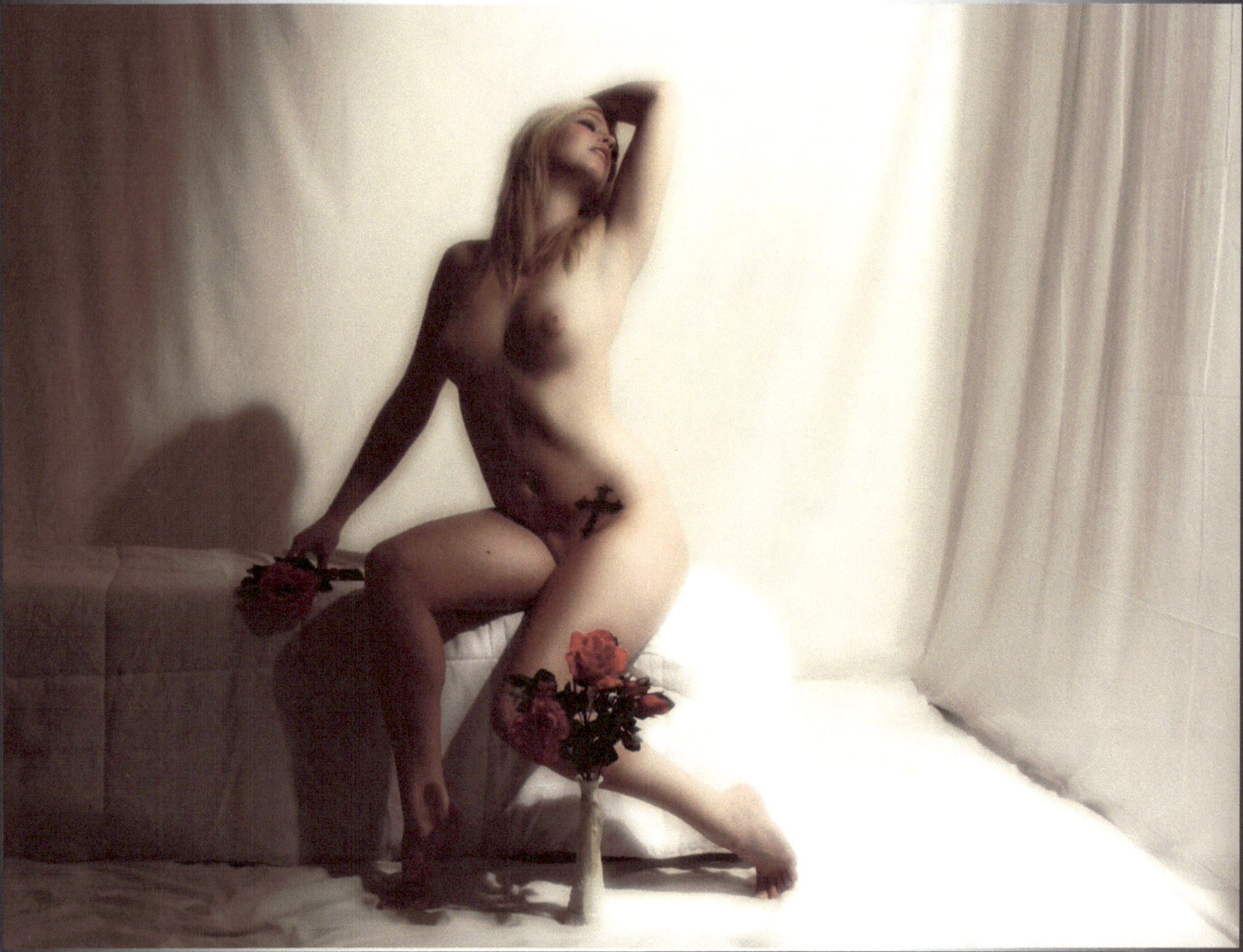

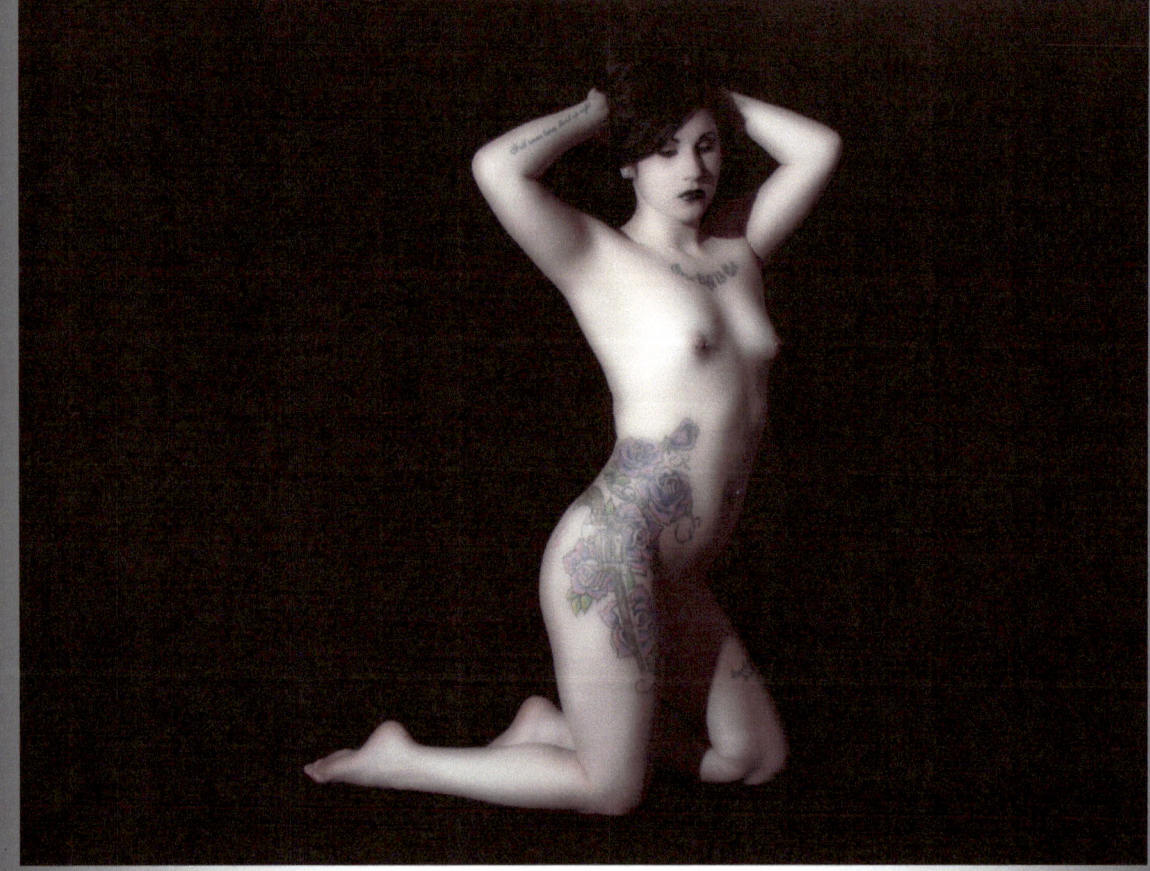

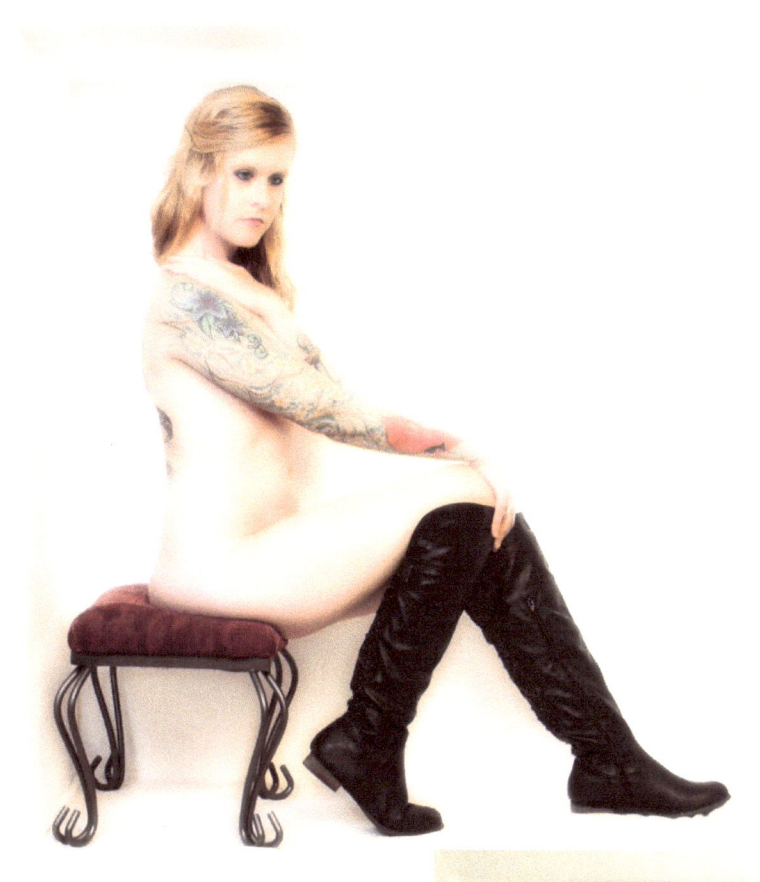
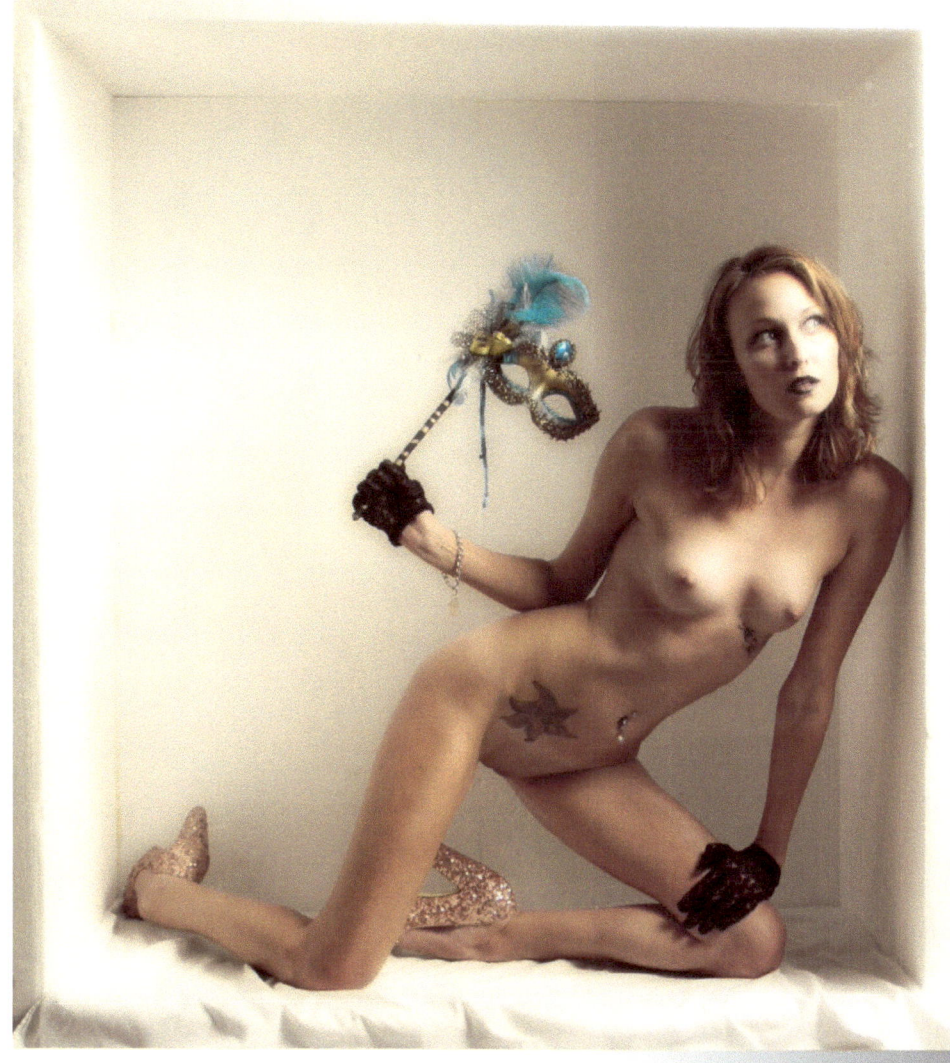

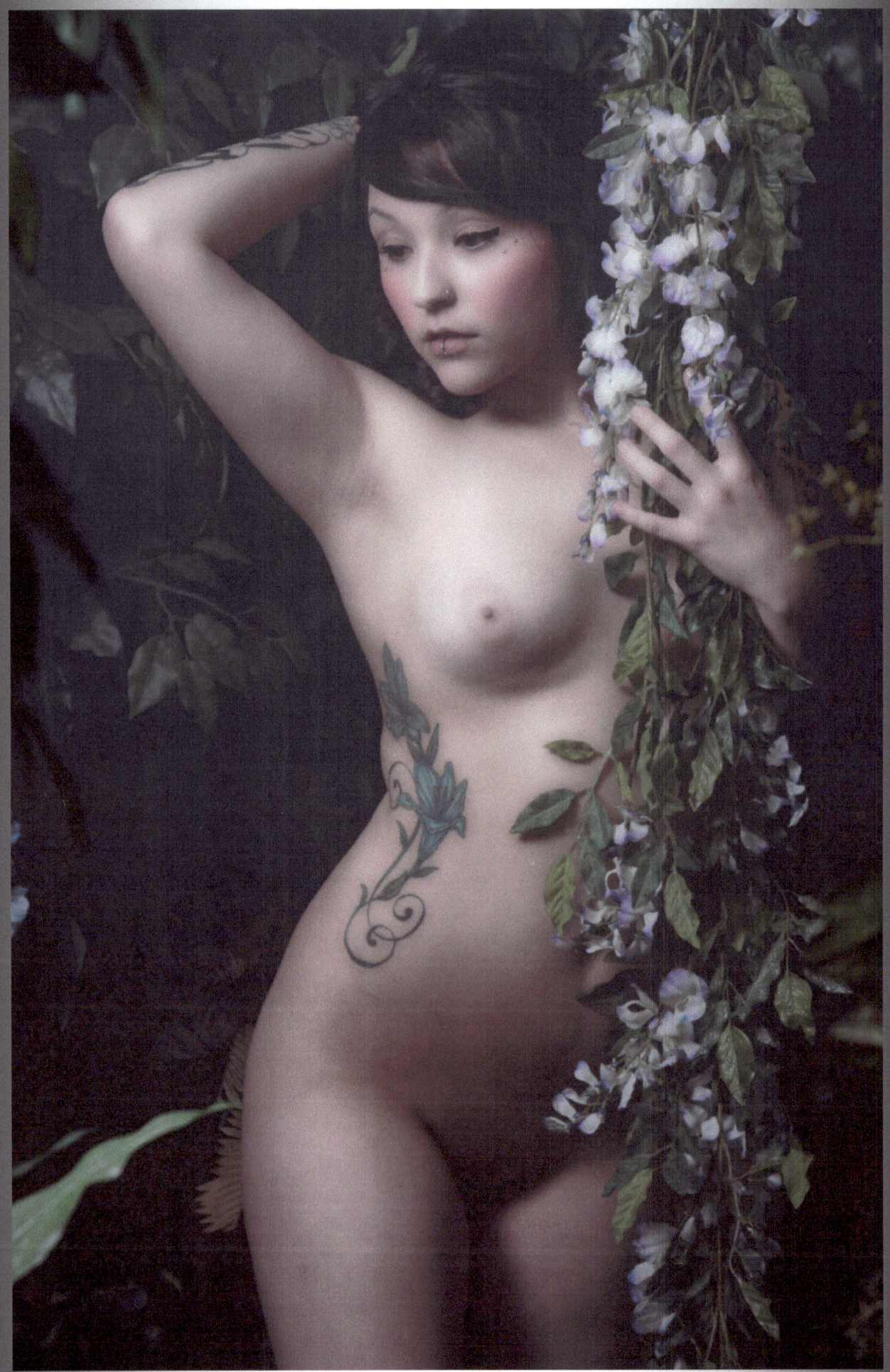

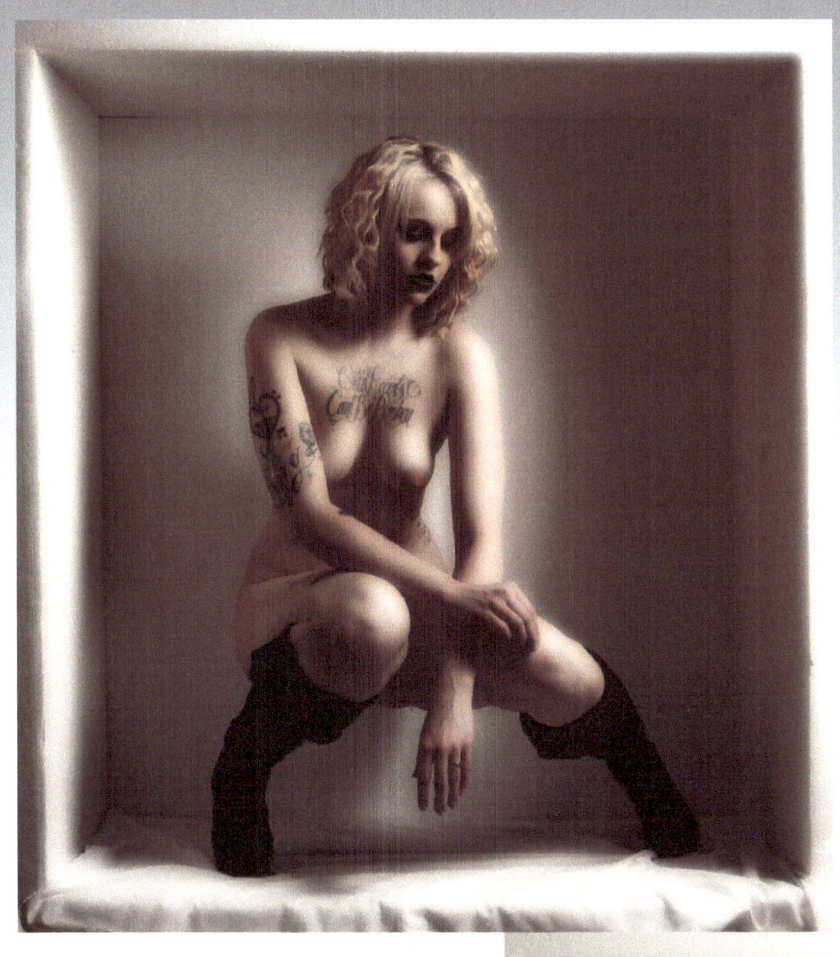
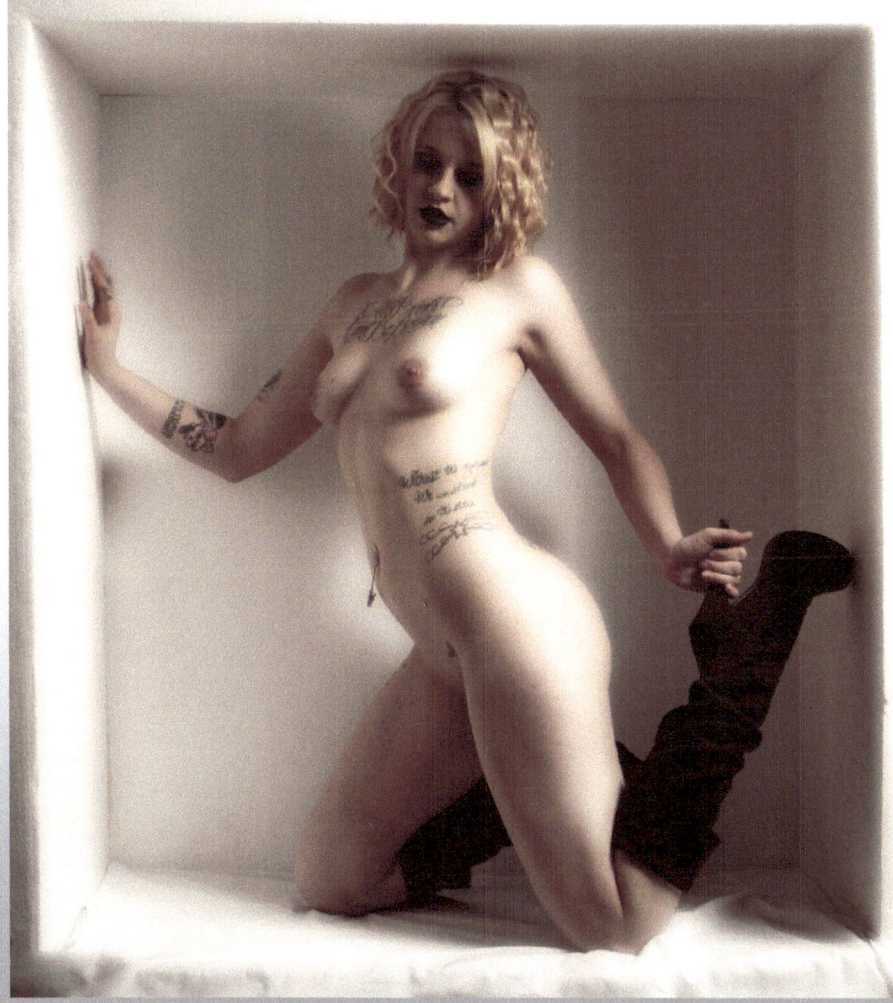

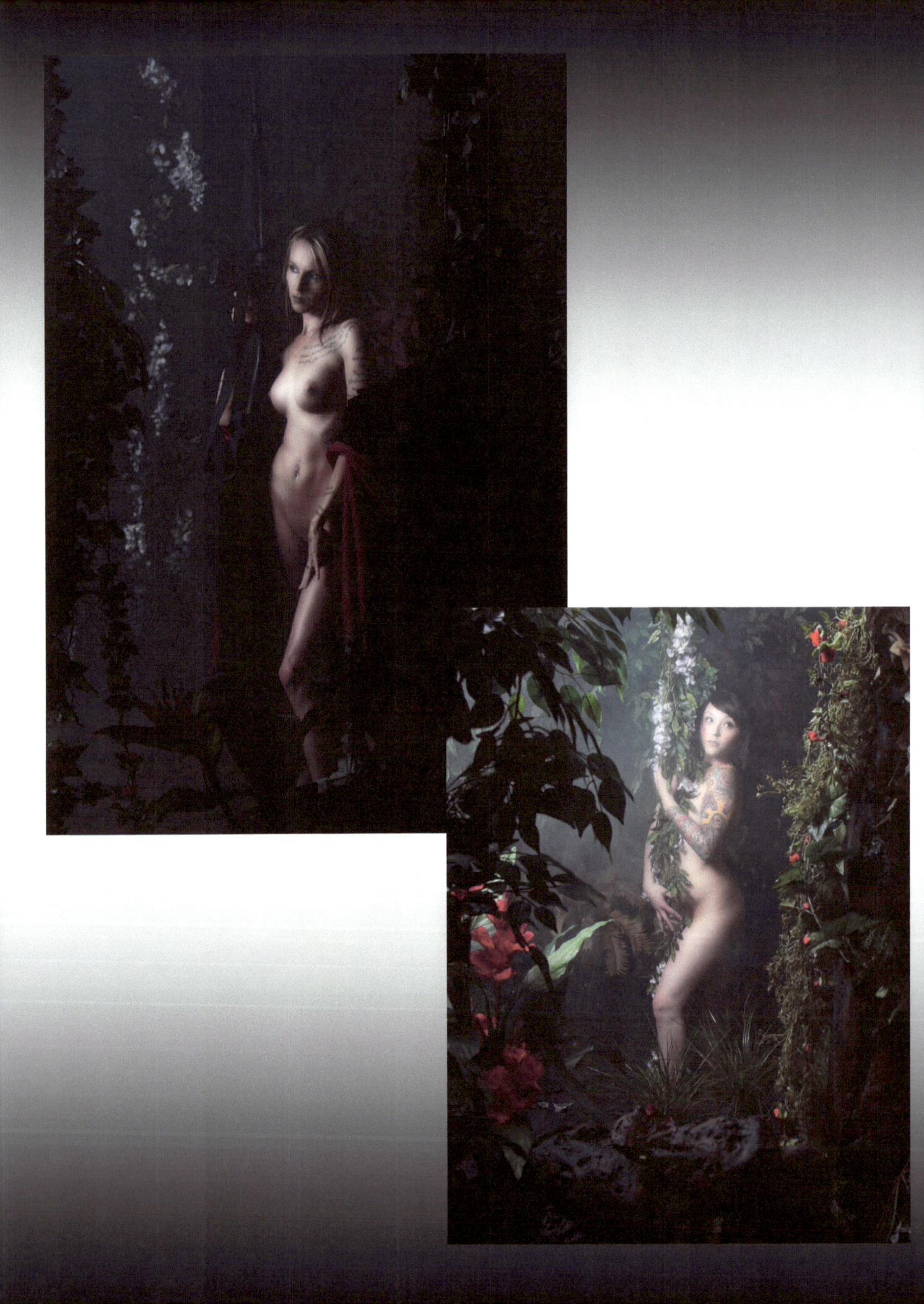

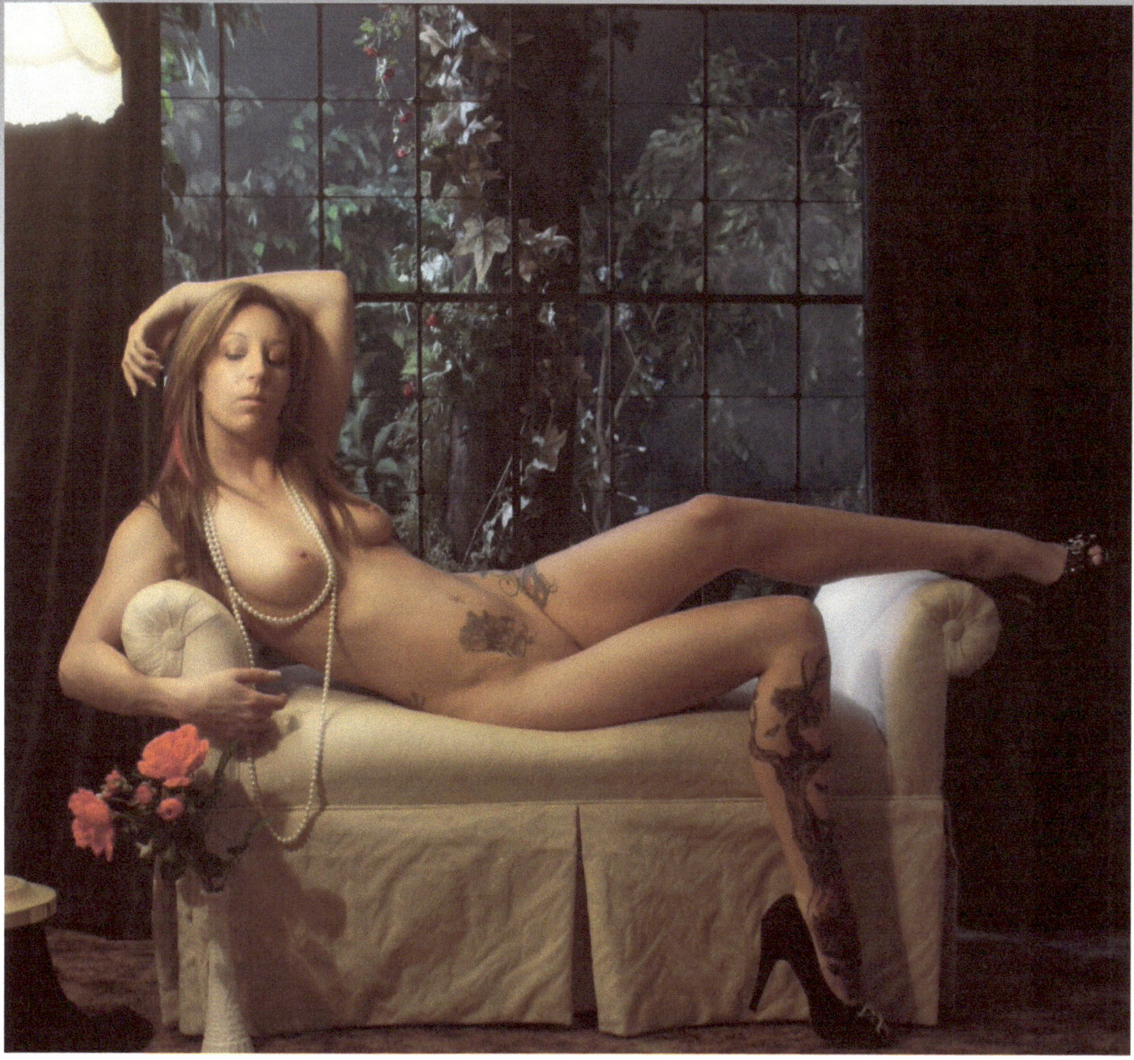

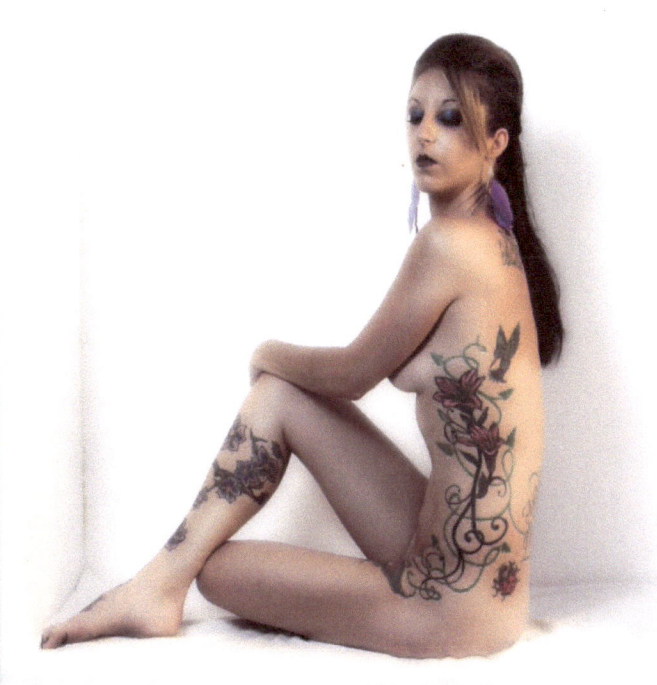

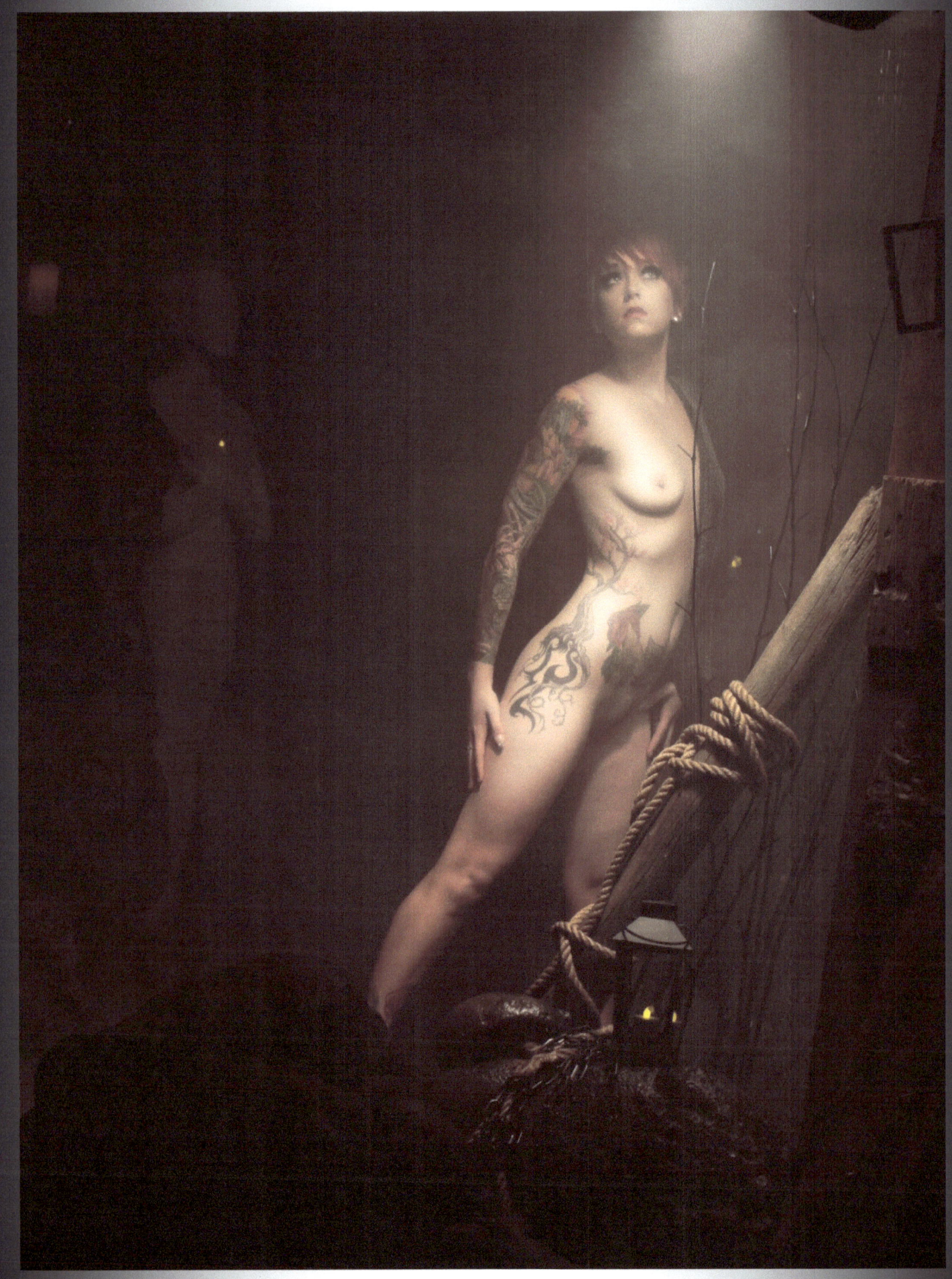

www.ingramcontent.com/pod-product-compliance
Lightning Source LLC
Chambersburg PA
CBHW050838180526
45159CB00004B/1948